A
MESSAGE
FROM
HIGHER
SOUL

The Human Experience from The Soul's Perspective

By Lee McKeown

First Printing: 2020

ISBN 978-0-244-56874-0

www.leemckeown.com

Table of Contents

Acknowledgments

This book is for all those who are awakening to who they truly are. Thank you from me, your angels, guides, and the universe for joining this invitation.

I just want to thank my family and friends for co-creating with me soul lessons so I can grow into the person I am now; I want to thank you for your love and support. I love you

I want to thank you all the beautiful souls who helped me put together is book, from design to structure and editing. I love you

I want to thank all those who have inspired me and motivated me over the years, to all the wonderful souls whom are carrying out their divine workings, to all the authors of the books I've read, to all the people whose documentaries I've watched. I love you

I want to thank myself for being on this journey, for being me may we continue to grow, evolve, love, laugh and inspire. I love you

I want to thank the universe, God, the angels, the ascended masters and HEBS of whom have channeled through me and worked with me day and night to bring this magical works to the consciousness of humanity. I love you

And finally, I want to thank you, for having the strength to step into your power, for taking your own learning and remembrance into your own hands. May this book re-spark your souls flame and awaken you to who you truly are, may this bring forth a new understanding in which you can understanding, forgive, heal and grow in ways you've always dreamed of.
I love you

Foreword

"Listen to what resonates in your heart and dismiss what which doesn't but listen closely for the heart never lies." — *Lee McKeown*

You will find throughout this book you will be encouraged to do your own research, this is because I don't want you to just blindly believe all that is speak about here, but to find your own truth, to allow your inner wisdom to speak to you.

You will also find words such as Great Spirit, Great Source, Infinite intelligence, the universe, all these are alternative words for God. This is because there have been so many different names given to God and also because due to core programming and religious propaganda people don't like to use the word God, as when you speak of God people immediately presume you are a part of organized religion which puts a lot of people off, or they simply dismiss it as much of humanity have been taught they are separate from God.

Where It Begins

The universe we live in is a mental universe. All beings are created by the thoughts and will of the Infinite Spirit. Just like with the Great Spirit, our physical realities are created by our thoughts, and it is the same for all in the universe. Everything in the world stems from the mind or consciousness of the Great Spirit. It has been known as many names, such as God, the Universe, and the Great Source. Despite the name, it is simply the divine consciousness that emanates through everything.

Everything within our realities is an extension of the same source. It's just that each is at their own level of vibration in accordance with the soul's current level of understanding and remembrance of that which it is. Each being has its own unique energy signature.

Everything is a vibration in a constant state of change and flow, meaning nothing rests. Rather, everything is evolving, including us.

Life, purpose, and destiny: what does it all mean? And what is the point of it? For years, religions have claimed to have the answer. For years, philosophers have claimed there is no answer. So, then what do we believe, or more to the point, what *should* we believe? What is real and what is not—or I should say, what is your truth and what is not?

For eons, those who wished to control humanity have fought, killed, and sacrificed life not only to stop you from discovering your true divine nature but also to get you to take on and follow their ideals or beliefs, to defend these beliefs, and to even kill for these beliefs so that you can help keep the status quo. So, the question that should be asked is this: is it your belief or a pre-programmed response to that which you have been told by others or simply perceived from others?

Beliefs are derived from repetitive thoughts. It's important to remember that beliefs do not reflect the actual experiences we have but are based on our perception of them, which are normally derived from programmed responses we have had, been told to have or observed in others, or possibly and in many cases brought forward from past lives.

Let's go back to life, purpose, and destiny and what it all means. We can agree that we have all had moments where we talk about the wonders of life and the universe, space, UFOs, the possibility of life on other planets, and the meaning of life with family or a group of friends only to go to sleep and forget all about it. We get caught up in our own drama, other people's drama, bills, money, relationships, sex, society, and the struggles of the world we face every day.

By now, you may be wondering, "Who in heavens is this guy?" so I'll tell you a little about me. But I don't want to put much focus on me as a person because the point of this book is the message, not the person. I am just like every other soul here on Earth—a three-part being consisting of a mind, a body, and a spirit. These components have been called many other names depending on the perspective, such as the subconscious, conscious, and superconscious. Despite the names, the message is the same. For all intents and purposes, we'll call them the trinity of the human makeup.

I'm thirty-two years old (in this lifetime) from a beautiful island called the United Kingdom. Like most I have had—or should say, chose—quite an eventful childhood. It maybe wasn't one out of a Disney fairy tale but one that prepared me for the understanding of who I am now, who I wish to be in my next moment, and what I'm here to do.

Like all souls, I have experienced immense darkness, as well as immense lightness, and there is a reason for this. (I will talk about that later, but for now, just keep it in mind.) For one to exist, there needs to be the other because together, they make a whole. So, for one to know oneself as light, for instance, one must experience darkness. If they didn't, the soul would have no reference point from which to create and, thus, couldn't know what it knows conceptually to be in the physical world. This may seem confusing, but don't worry. We will go into more detail later.

I don't like to use judgments such as good or bad. Why? Because, as we've already briefly discussed, for one thing to exist, the opposite must also exist, so in essence good and bad are the same but different in degree. This is the same with everything in life. It must be both because it's part of the creation and governed by universal law. But again, we ask the question, how can one know the experience of good if one has never had experience of bad? One would not have a reference point from which to draw. Just like hot and cold, light and dark, all are the same except that they vary in degrees, and the same can be said about good and bad, So you see, as with all experience of polarity and duality, they are not separate but a part of the whole experience. However, for the purpose of deeper understanding, I may refer to these labels to help you have a clearer understanding of what I'm saying.

From a limited human perspective, one might classify my childhood as bad, traumatic, or distressing. But as I say, it was neither good nor bad. It was what it was. Ultimately, it was one of many chosen experiences causing soul growth and remembrance to bring me closer to the vibration of divine love.

Before I continue, I want to say that I hold no resentment, anger, or grudges against anyone. I forgive everyone. I love my parents to the fullness of my heart and forgive them. I bless every experience and situation I have had with and without them and with anyone I have connected to within my life, be it what one might call a bad experience or a good experience.

Let's continue.

In my childhood, I experienced a lot of violence, aggression, drug and alcohol abuse, and a general lack of love. I am not saying that my parents didn't love me, my sister, or my brother because they did as best, they could. We all chose some of our experiences before coming to Earth, but I guess you could say my parents had a lot of things going on, a lot of experiences they chose to have to grow and develop.

At the age of six and seven, I was taken into foster care with my brother. People may say this is sad, but at the time, it was needed. We all needed to get away from that environment. Plus, it was what my brother, my sister, my parents, and I and all else who were involved chose. Maybe not on a physical level but on a soul level.

After moving from place to place, my brother and I finally settled in permanent placement in Telford, Shropshire, with a beautiful family called the Wakelams. Beryl was my foster mother, and Ray was my foster dad. There we stayed until I was eighteen years old.

I haven't always been this spiritual person. (Or have I?) In fact, I have only been consciously aware of my spiritual aspect and soul purpose for about ten years. Although I will say this (and some of you may relate): I have always felt different. Ever since I was a child, I felt confused, like Earth wasn't my home, always seen as a strange child or an outcast, confused by the "human" ways. I guess you could say I knew back then that I was here for a reason. But like most who incarnate or reincarnate here on Earth, these thoughts I pondered quickly dissipated, getting what I like to call "integrated" into the illusion of the human experience. I was trying to live up to society's standards and do my best to fit in. But no matter how hard I tried, it just didn't resonate with me and caused much self-abuse and destruction.

Don't get me wrong. I had and still have a great circle of friends who love and respect me, and I love and respect them too. I just always chose to stand at the back whenever I was in a group when most wanted to be seen, to be the leader or the alpha male of the pack. I just wanted to settle nicely in the middle.

So yes, of the several schools I attended, I loved and was loved, but beneath it all, I still felt alien-like, sensing that Earth wasn't my home of homes. I was always being called "strange" or "weird." I mean, I could step into a room, not say a word, and still be told I was strange or not normal, which used to make me feel outcast, uncomfortable, and at times, upset. But I can say that I also perceived humans and their ways as strange and weird. Now I know and understand why. Now that I've accepted that I may be a little "different," I love it. I love me and who I am, embracing my divine side and my unique views and energy.

By the time I was thirteen, I was well and truly integrated into the illusion of the human experience, getting drunk with friends, smoking cannabis—or "wacky backy," as my foster mom used to call it, bless her. I was just doing what any curious adolescent boy would do.

It was around this time that I picked up the guitar, something I had always wanted to do, ever since I was a kid watching my dad strum away. As my interest in music increased, my interest in school decreased. It wasn't that I wasn't interested in what the teachers had to say. It was just that what
 was being told to me wasn't my truth in my heart of hearts. Or maybe that was just my way justifying my rebelliousness and lack of participation in the system. Either way, I struggled with school.

By the age of sixteen, I was well and truly a wannabe rocker, growing my hair, wearing ripped jeans and baggy tops, listening to all sorts of rock music but mainly grunge and indie (at that time). I was still smoking, still curious, and still confused about the world around me.

From the ages of sixteen to twenty-one, I had a few relationships and a couple of heavy ones, but again, they did not last. I struggled with living up to other people's expectations, not to mention that I was still heavy on drugs, and my heart had been a closed off due to my past experiences. I felt like I just couldn't give people the love they wanted. Looking back, you could say I couldn't love myself either.

I will say this: even if I wasn't at the time, I now am truly grateful and blessed for every person and relationship I have had, be it good or bad. They developed my soul understanding and my self-understanding, as well as my understanding of divine love. So, to all of you, from my heart to yours, thank you!

At the age of eighteen, I came out of the foster care system and moved into an apartment with my girlfriend at the time. However, due to my heavy drug use and other personal issues going on at that time, we split up.

Music was my life, I spent most my days writing songs, playing songs, and managing the band I had put together. I lived, breathed, and strived so hard to become a rich and famous rock star, but I always said I never wanted fame, just to tour the world and play my songs to the world. As I said earlier, I was very much sucked into the illusion of life, wanting what the TV told me I wanted but mainly acting out of ego and fear. I didn't care for much and only really cared about my looks, drugs, sex, and women, always looking to get my next hit.

Oops! I forgot to say that my lack of love for myself and confusion about life had gotten worse, and so my outer world reflected that. My "wacky backy" habit had taken the next step to many other drugs, and I was taking basically whatever I could get my hands on. Looking back, I thought it was because I liked the feeling, but the truth is that I was hiding from the struggles of my past and being on Earth, including the frustration of failed relationships, the constantly struggle to make ends meet, and the fact that the band was just not moving anywhere. Don't get me wrong. The band had a lot of hype around it, but anytime we were close to a record signing or hitting it big, something would come up. This situation was demoralizing for me, so the more alcohol and drugs I took, the less sense life made to me. My confusion about my purpose here was increasing, and the familiar feeling of wanting to go home was getting to be all too much to handle.

Eventually, I got to a suicidal state. Everything just got to be too much, so one night, when I was under the influence of drugs and alcohol, distraught, and at my wit's end, I took a knife in my hands. Feeling tired and ready to end it all, I dropped to my knees and shouted, "If there is a God, listen to me! What is my purpose here? Why is life so harsh? Why are people so hateful?" I ranted and let it all out. Exhausted and feeling tired and cried out, I dropped the knife, went to bed, and forgot all about it, but the Great Spirit didn't. From there, everything changed.

Soon after that night, in my early 20's, I found that my passion for songwriting and music started to dwindle. My heart had started to take a new profound direction. The band wasn't satisfying me anymore.

One of my previous band members and angel in disguise came along and gifted me from the heavens my first book on consciousness. Looking back, I can see that the book was a major trigger of my awakening, the remembering of who I am, and the discovery of what my purpose is.

I read the book over and over. I was hooked. What it spoke of just rang true in my heart, and it changed my life forever. I began to make some of the changes the book suggested. As I started to raise my vibration, so to speak, my habits changed also.

From there onwards, I read more and more books and started watching all sorts of things on the internet: conspirators, aliens, new world order (NOW), physics, space, angels, religion, energy, God, and the devil. You name it, I read it, I watched it. What was strange most about what I was digesting was that it didn't feel new to me. It didn't feel like nonsense, which now I know is because I wasn't learning but just remembering. After all, the Earth is the school of remembrance, not learning, as we have been told.

My social life changed, and the people I hung around with changed. I stopped all drugs and started to go to the gym, which, if you knew me back then, would have been a shock itself. My diet changed, my dress sense changed, the way I spoke and conducted myself changed, and my overall personality and character changed. One of the biggest changes was my love for myself, people and my ever-increasing connection with spirit and the angels, ascended masters, and my heart space. I was slowly becoming aware of my inner power and my energy.

I bought oracle cards to help deepen my connection with my personal guides and angels.

I started to feel my angels', guides', and ascended masters' presence, seeing more and more signs, such as flashing lights and light-headedness. I'd always experienced these sensations, but I just thought it was due to low blood sugar levels like the doctor said when I was a child. I also started noticing universal synchronicities, which we term "coincidences." But as I studied more about life and spirit, I started to understand there is no such thing as a coincidence, but we'll go into that later.

From then on, I focused on my inner self and connecting deeper with that forgotten aspect of myself: the soul. I spent all my time focusing on my soul and its purpose here, bringing balance among my mind, body, and spirit. I lived in gratitude and joy and in meditation, connecting with the angels and talking to and strengthening my connection with the Divine and my higher self.

All of this has led me to who I am today and, most importantly, who I chose to be, which has allowed me to help many other people on their journeys of remembrance.

Despite all the self-destruction and drugs, people have always been drawn to me. They would always open up to me and tell me their deepest emotions and feelings, and I would pull out some amazing advice. I would often say to whoever I was speaking to, "I don't know where that comes from." Now I do.

So that was a little about me. Now about the book.

This book is a book for people of all ages who feel like they have a purpose in life (which we all do) but are unsure about what it is. It is for those who want to experience a new way of living, those who have felt and heard the call, those who don't resonate with the ways of humanity, for those who want answers, those who have called out for guidance, and those who want to help Mother Earth. It's for people who want to move towards an experience of Divine love rather than fear and ego. It's for those who wish to make their dreams a reality, those who wish to be the change they see the world, those who want to awaken or trigger a soul remembrance, and those who want to discover the Divine truth of who they are and what we are doing here.

Before we get into this book, I must ask that you please don't blindly believe everything I've written here. If you did, you wouldn't be not uncovering your own truth. Instead, listen to what words resonate in your heart because all Divine truths and answers lie there, and the heart never lies.

Remember what I said earlier about beliefs? A true stage of knowing is embodiment. You won't need to know if something is true, nor will you need to prove or explain. You will feel its resonance deep within. As you read this book, it will cause your heart to open. You will become it, it will echo through your energy, and it will be integrated into your everyday life, which will be plain to see by any observer.

Your angels are always with you, and they love you dearly no matter what acts you have performed, what words you may have spoken, be they "good" or "bad," or what thoughts you've had, again be they "good" or "bad." They know of the difficulties here on this dense Earth plane. They are so proud of you and love you completely, and they invite you to see the same in yourself. They want you to know you are protected and guided, and they only want for you what you want, and that is to live a life of your grandest joy through a heart in peace, unity, love, and understanding.

The angels and the Great Spirit thank you for accepting this invitation and want to let you know that you have arrived right on time, just like you agreed.

If you wanted or asked for a sign of confirmation or heaven communication, here it is, just as it appeared to me as I sat here writing these words. Know that you are a part of the body of the Great Divine, you are a perfect idea in the mind of the Great Spirit, and your angels and the Universe are all rejoicing in this golden age of remembrance and Divine love. It is the Divine and my will and hope is that you get from this book that which you seek or called for.

Everything in this book is not "fact" but my perspective based on my experiences and inner wisdom, as well as the messages and statements brought forth to me from ascended masters and the angels. I hope that you remember who you truly are, start to go within and bring remembrance of who you are to reveal the Divine gifts we all have, start consciously creating your human experience to become the cause of life and not the unconscious effect, and share that with the world, in turn helping mother Gaia to ascend as she helps us.

Life, Its Meaning and Purpose

Life is an endless cycle and rhythm of creation and change, the ebb and flow of cosmic space. It is co-created by us and the Great Spirit so it and we can know and create in the physical world what we know to be conceptually in the spirit world and reflect out here and now what we have remembered and know to be based on our own perspectives gained from our various experiences in previous lives.

The soul blueprint and karmic factors are all considered by the soul before creating its "soul lessons" and its current human experience. Ultimately, experiences are created to remind the soul of its divine nature and essence and create it in the physical, embodying one's forgotten Divine essence of Divine love into the human physical experience. It's the part of us that sees and feels compassion, unity, forgiveness, understanding, joy, and happiness—the part that was created by love and allows us to create. It's the oneness that we truly are and all that truly is. Life3 gives us a blank canvas on which to create through consciousness events and experience we desire, although due to the repression of Divine truth we may be doing this all subconsciously.

For years, we have dismissed this idea that thoughts create things despite many great masters and guru's showing us otherwise. We go through life thinking life is simply a bunch of random events and situations created by someone else with no meaning and that we have no purpose with only one certainty: we die. What is the point of living just to die? Why get a job? Why bother with relationships if we're just going to lose them anyway? Why incarnate or reincarnate onto this Earth plane with all its stresses and strains of living up to society's morals and expectations, being told what to think, where to be, and what to do, all programming us with beliefs that aren't our own? We are told what love is, what to fear, what to eat, what is acceptable, what is not, and what success is. We are brainwashed into giving our permission to the monetary system, from which only a few seem to benefit and have control of all Earth's resources, banks, corporations, governments, militaries, and surveillance, trying at every turn to turn us into automated consuming robots. We are led to the thought that if life has no meaning, then neither do we.

This reality is an illusion. The Mayans called it "*Maya*." Regardless of what we have all been told to believe, the human life experience is not about what you have, where you live, whether you're financially successful, how many houses you have, how many people love you, how others perceive you, nor any other material possession. Life is about the soul and its evolution. The soul only cares about what you chose to be at any given moment in relation to who you believe you are. This materialistic illusion is a distortion, one meant to keep us spending, keep us controlled, and ultimately keep us distracted from remembering who we truly are and the Divine gifts we all have. The powers that be know if we all awaken to our true potential, their hold over humanity would cease to exist.

Life is about the soul and soul growth through physical experience. It's called an illusion because we have been taught to believe that the human experience is about the materialistic world when, in fact, it's far from it. It's not what we have and what we don't but how we to relate to the experience from a gained perspective and, thus, a newly gained perspective by using Divine love and our essence as a reference point and raising our vibration.

The purpose of soul's evolution on earth is to grow in self-mastery, to heal and balance your karma, fulfill your mission on earth in accordance with your soul plan/blueprint and to ascend higher in the Light.

It's simply a game of giving and receiving—that is, giving and receiving through understanding Divine love. But before you can understand this, you must understand Divine or Universal law and how these laws influence your life experience, which I'll get into later in the book. Once you develop an understanding of your essence and how the laws work in conjunction with your experience, you will be able to unlock the key to your soul and the Universe.

It's about us, —the human beings—the evolution and consciousness growth of each soul's essence and the collective and overcoming our personal and collective fears and transmuting them with love and universal understanding. Only when we overcome all fears can we all truly ascend and be free.

Where We Begin

The soul and essence come from the spirit plane, after discussing and organizing with other souls, your spirit guides, and angels (who we will speak about later in this book). It forms a blueprint, a type of plan, about what it wishes to experience and what will cause soul growth, taking in to account previous life experiences and karmic energy. Nothing in life we face is meant to be against us but simply to develop a soul understanding of who we truly are and bring us back to Divine love.

For the soul to grow and remember what it is, we chose and agreed to have certain experiences. These experiences are created by you and for you but also for others. These souls could be partners, friends, enemies, acquaintances, or work colleagues.

I believe that angels come in many forms, not just as figures with wings made of light. Angels can come in the form of humans. We all come from the same Great Source of Divine consciousness, so greet all as angels because they come to us as a gift from the heavens, and yes, that includes those you classify as enemies or bad people. Regardless of the label we give, and all are here with us to help us grow and heal, and we are here to help them grow and heal.

We incarnate or reincarnate into a physical vessel we call the human body depending on the nature of the soul. But let's get something straight: we are not a body with a soul as has been impressed upon us. We are, in fact, a soul with a body.

For eons, science and religion have argued over this question have still not come to a conclusion, as with many things when it comes to religion and science.

The first stage of reincarnation is a review of the soul's past life or lives, the creation of the soul blueprint, and the choosing of parents and certain experiences. Then, we are birthed into the physical vessel. We then live a life that we decide how long it will be—yes, we choose our so-called deaths or passing, as I like to call it. We live out our soul plan, and thus, the human experience begins.

I watched an amazing documentary about reincarnation. It featured a little boy who, at the age of six or seven, remembered his past life. He remembered being an army pilot and, more interestingly, going through the process of picking his parents before inhabiting his physical vessel. To the parent's surprise, the little boy told them that he flew to them and saw them making love and having sex through the window. He told them about the room they were in, what it looked like, and the location. He turned them into believers! It was no surprise to find that the boy was also a strong intuitive.

We forget who we truly are through Divine design and the Great Forgetting. Why must we forget our whole Divine perfection? Why would a soul come to Earth and experience the struggles and hardships? Why wouldn't it just stay in the heavens in bliss and peace? Because there, in it all, it cannot truly experience what it is unto itself, so it needs to have experiences with others as a reference point. If a soul came to Earth with all its remembrance, then it would have no reason to be here; a soul only comes to Earth to create the perfection of what it knows itself conceptually to be on the soul plane in the physical world. If a soul remembered what it truly was from birth, well, then it wouldn't need to be born. It wouldn't need to have experiences to help promote Divine remembrance. It would just simply be pointless.

There have been a few masters who retained their Divine remembrance, which again, doesn't occur at birth but gets triggered at a later age. Regardless, these masters show up to remind us that we are the embodiment of the same source they are. They are not there to be worshipped. Master Jesus was one, and as he once said, "What I can do, you can do too." None of these so-called gods came down to be worshiped but to be an inspiration in the hope of re-sparking that inner soul knowledge and inspiring you to discover your own truth and live a life embodied by that truth. That is another reason that souls like this get attacked and ridiculed—these souls are a threat to the status quo. Whether they are ascended masters or just highly intuitive, awakened human souls, these beings are seen as a threat to the status quo because they promote love for all, whereas the system in place promotes fear for all.

It was never about the person but the message.

In short, a soul goes from perfection (the spirit world) to non-perfection (the human experience) back to perfection, and so it is forever.

Why would you choose to reincarnate into what seems like such a violent and hard experience? The reason we choose to come to Earth is the amazing diversity of experiences available here due to duality and polarity. The thing that makes Earth such an enticing place for a soul is the fact it is a free-will system and one of a unique design that enables us to have a path but also the free will to divert and go our own ways. This setup is not the way it is everywhere in the universe and is why the world is the way we see it now, and why it is in the state and vibration it is now. It is also why we have such diversity in our beliefs, ways of living, ideas, thoughts, and morals. This diversity offers souls more experiences in one place, offering greater lessons and grander remembrance of who you truly are and who you wish to be. Earth may seem difficult to the physical being, your soul absolutely loves it here, and that is why it keeps coming back.

The Message about the Meaning of Life

Life and the human experience is simply a mental creation through the mind of the Great Spirit, who works through you and with you so that you might remember that you are pure, unconditional, non-judgmental Divine love and so that you create and express that in your physical reality through the power of thought, faith, and belief. We have this Earth experience so that we might physically know what we think ourselves to be through life experiences. As we go through our many incarnations and physical experiences, we learn more about our true essence, slowing climbing up the ascension ladder so that we will eventually find our way back to the heart of God, or as the bible says "back home to God"

We all have a path—a soul blueprint which I will be talking of later—but then the free will to follow or not follow that exact path. We asked for and created the lives we are experiencing right now so that we might uncover our divine heritage and express our divine gifts to better not only the individual experience but also the collective. The ultimate goal is to remember that you are a part of the body of the Great Spirit and to express that pure Divine love essence in your reality for yourself and as a beacon for others so that they remember and express the love that they are, so we can collectivity bring forth through consciousness creativity a new world, a new way of living where the focus is soul and love and not ego and fear.

Soul wants you to know and remember that you are not here by accident, you are here for a reason and a purpose. You chose this life you are currently experiencing all to help you to evolve in the understanding of your divine heritage.

You live many lives this life is not the only one, you play many roles in life, this chosen by you simply because your soul wants to feel and experience all the physical world has to offer including that which seems from a human perspective to be bad.

You are not here to worship anyone, but you realize the divinity in yourself and worship that part of you.

Soul gets given a preview of what energies and experience on may face when in the physical, but this doesn't mean it can predict all the events created when it's in the physical realm.

The Soul

In the previous chapter, we gained a basic understanding of the reason for this process that we call "life" or "the human experience." But what is a soul? Philosophers, religions, and science have argued about this question for eons, and it is still argued about to this day without a consensus.

The soul is the idea of you in the mind of the Infinite Spirit. You are here because you are an infinite idea in the divine mind, the Great Spirit is always thinking about you. Isn't that a beautiful thought?

The "me" presence, and relates to the physical world such as job role, character and often identifies with the mind and ego, whereas the soul is your "I am" presence meaning the part of you which is a incarnation of the individualized presence of God or Great Spirit also known as your "higher self", It is your true individual self which cannot not die, I will be speaking about this later on but I just wanted to touch upon it now, you are not a body with a soul but in fact a soul with a body. The body because it's made of material substances can decompose and so in a sense does "die", but the soul cannot die as it is simply energy and as we know energy can't be destroyed it simply transforms. The idea of death as we have been taught is a distortion of the truth. The soul is immortal.

The soul is your very essence, what makes you, you, and what keeps you breathing. It is the Divine energy (light) within each and every one of us that is connected to the All. It a fragmented part of the whole—that which we call God or the Great Spirit—that has chosen to separate itself from itself to create and physically experience that which it is formed from and its conception of who it thinks it is. It is only through physical experience of what soul knows itself to be, that it can in fact know itself to be. This is because when on the spirit plane there is only pure consciousness, and so soul can only know what it thinks it is through consciousness and not physical experience. God wants your soul to realize its oneness with itself, that's all God wants and so co- creates as you and with you, your physical experiences where soul can manifest its God like essence. It is the physical experience which brings soul to its full and complete understanding of its divine nature.

The soul chose many different roles in its incarnations from a king to a peasant, from a man to a woman, from a parent of a soul, to a child of that same soul. Soul loves to experience all it can and by switching roles it allows it to gain deeper understanding and wisdom. So make no mistake you have played the rich person, the poor person, you have played the king and the queen, you have been the university student and the homeless person, you have been the hero and you have been the villain, because from each role comes a new experience which in turn creates a new perspective which then creates new understandings which then also creates new soul remembrance of the true divine self.

The soul is the part of us that controls our experiences and creations and is the only reason we can create. It is the main reason why we find ourselves in this current lifecycle or human experience. It is the part of us we have long forgotten. It is the part of us that inhabits the physical vessel (body) and allows us to breathe, move, and use our senses. It is that part of us that often guides us through intuition (a.k.a., gut feeling). It is the part of us that sees no judgment and no separation but only oneness, connected to everything in the Universe's cosmic web. It's the part of us that is connected to the high realms, the angels, the ascended masters, and above all, your higher self.

The soul is the reason we sleep and dream. It is the reason we differ from one another but also why we are similar. It is the reason we live and feel and the reason why we may find ourselves in a certain situation with certain people, whether it's perceived from a limited human perspective as good or bad. It is the reason we have the ability and imagination to create amazing pieces of art, beautiful poetry, and all creative arts; creativity derives from the soul aspect of the human experience.

The soul is the reason we breathe and the reason we love. The soul is our one true essence, the part of us that is connected to the whole world and universe, the part of us that knows all, and the part of us that is co-creating your experience with Great Spirit is this moment.

Everything in the universe has and is soul experiencing. Yes, from a grain of sand to a big blue whale, no matter how big or small, everything is part of the All. Everything is choosing what it wishes to experience in every moment to grow and expand spiritual knowledge of itself and what it truly is.

This may be profound to hear, but scientists have done many experiments to prove that all particles, at their subatomic levels, have intelligence—yes, even a grain of sand is choosing to be just that—and that objects we deem to be solid are found not to be so under a microscope.

So that I don't get sidetracked, I will leave that there, but if you want to know more then, do your own investigation. There are many resources out there explaining this finding, as well as many other subjects I will be talking about. I ask you just bear in mind that everything chooses what it wishes to be and what it wishes to become.

Don't take my word for it. Take responsibly for your learning and start digging......or not.

In the modern world, the soul isn't really talked about, acknowledged, or even believed to exist, even though religion, philosophers, scientists, and master thinkers have agreed for centuries that there is soul. But like many of the grand truths that have been passed down to us over the years, this truth has been purposely distorted to keep us in a low state of consciousness in which we are easy to control and manipulate.

I could go deeper and expand further, but the point of this book is to keep the message simple. If you do want to do your own research, then feel free again to do it and discern for yourself.

The Message about The Soul

Your soul is the "I am" presence, the individualized incarnation of God. It holds all the answers and wisdom one may be searching for.

The soul cannot die.

Soul is the extension of the God.

The Soul has lived many lifetimes, maybe not just earth but often on other planets and in other universes. It is not the mind that is the deciding factor when it comes to major life decisions but the soul.

It is our true vessel for which we are truly experiencing through. It is simply on a mission to rediscover who it truly is in the physical by expressing its divinity through the power of love energy vibration and creative consciousness, which through every experience and lesson gained moves it one step closer back home to understanding and wholeness of the Great Spirit.

The soul is the idea of you in the mind of God or Great Spirit. Despite what the Western world teaches, we are a soul with a body, and the soul is the true aspect of your essence and human makeup, in fact it is the soul factor which created the person you are now, the way you look, the experiences you have, the way you think and the way you perceive both internal and external worlds.

The soul only cares about what you are being, not what you have. It just wants to feel it's true and experience its true nature being love joy happiness, but above that, to expand your consciousness and express your true essence (Divine love) in the physical so that you can move closer to the mind of the All, the mind of the Great Creator.

Soul Age

The path or life experience a soul chooses and finds itself experiencing on Earth all depends on where the soul has been, where it has come from, and where it is within its spiritual understanding and the journey home. Which brings us to soul age.

Have you ever met someone or hung around with someone who's older than you but seems and acts younger than you? Or met a younger person who seems to have more mental maturity than most in their age range? Well, this is because of soul age. What is soul age?

When talking about soul age, we may refer to terms such as "old," "mature," "young," and so on, but we aren't talking about age as we know it here on Earth.

We were all created at the Big Bang—the great separation. "Soul age" is a term used to discuss the basic idea of where a soul is with its spiritual understanding, which it has obtained over lifetimes, in regards to who and what it truly is and how fast it wishes to remember who it really is.

All souls that incarnate or reincarnate on Earth have a seventh-dimensional spiritual understanding within their soul makeup. All souls have with this wisdom stored within the light body. However, due to the Great Forgetting and the design of Earth, most souls were not or are not ready to access this sacred knowledge in the third dimension. The souls at this level of understanding and can access their sacred soul heritage and tend to be the cosmic seeds. But what are cosmic seeds?

While all souls are star seeds, not all souls on Earth have had incarnation on other planets, in other galaxies, or in other dimensions. Only certain souls here on Earth chose to have many experiences elsewhere. These souls are what I call cosmic seeds.

To better understand soul age and the difference between star seeds and cosmic seeds, think of the birth of stars. While all stars were created at the same moment, some stars chose to birth earlier and some later. It is the same with human souls. Some souls chose to birth themselves earlier, and others later. That is how we have different soul ages.

Cosmic seeds are the souls who chose to be birthed at an earlier time, so to speak, and who chose more experiences on many different planets and planes. This choice enabled them to gain a deeper knowledge and understanding of their soul heritage and allows a deeper connection with their spirit angels and guides.

Most but not all souls on Earth have chosen to reincarnate at a later stage than those of cosmic seeds. Because of this choice and because they have only experienced the planet Earth and this dimension alone, they tend to be younger in their knowledge of cosmic wisdom. These souls tend to be the mature, young, infant, and baby souls here now in terms of their understanding of their soul heritage and spiritual understandings.

While we may have different souls birthed at different times, when it comes to experiences and uncovering of sacred knowledge, all souls start at the bottom of the spiritual ladder despite being cosmic seeds or star seeds and work their way up to the older stages. Just because a soul may be an old soul at this moment, it does not mean that it is above a young soul. It simply means that that soul took a quicker path to the remembrance of who they truly are, quite often to help those souls who are lost or struggling remember. Most cosmic seeds chose a path to become masters of the universe or intergalactic healers, but ultimately, we all have and will reach the old soul stage—a.k.a. a higher level of knowing spiritual heritage and understandings. We will all make it back home to God or the Great Spirit.

Although we are all at a different point in our journeys and remembrance of who we are here on Earth, we all have the capacity to reach a fifth-level spiritual understanding, as mentioned previously—and more so now as we again go through the golden age, allowing us as souls to double shift from third- to fifth-dimensional vibrations and allowing souls to skip certain soul age stages, rather than taking it one step at a time, as it has been in past times gone by. We can jump from a young soul to an old, for instance.

Now, this is where it may get a bit confusing but bear with me. All will become clear.

You may be asking why some souls would choose many experiences in other places, galaxies, and dimensions when others just choose one planet of experience. Here is what the angels told me:

The souls who came to Earth and have only had Earth experiences did not do make this choice on purpose. The way Earth was created and set up was with a new creation: free will. The souls wanted to experience this free will without being aware of the issues they may face in the beginning. The problem was that when the souls came here, they totally forgot their essence and the purpose of life, but still held knowledge of the divine gifts they held, because of the forgetting of their true essence they started to experiment with their gifts but in a more perverse and destructive way.

Due to the newly created idea of free will, the souls started to do as they pleased. They started to go against their very Divine nature and started creating things that were not of pure Divine essence (which is still happening now), which in turn created cosmic karma, which they needed to heal here on Earth before they could leave which souls are still doing today.

Earth is also one of the shortest experiences a soul has in a lifetime, so a soul is still a child regarding itself Divine knowing. In many cases, before a soul has reached any form of higher understanding, its experience would be over, and it would die (as we label it here). It would have to continually reincarnate and start over from scratch. But each time it did, it would climb one step further in their understanding. This process is a very slow and long process, which is why humans are called "children of God."

In the beginning, Earth was created as an experiment and held a high vibration energy field or grid. It was also the only planet with the law of free will, meaning that you had not only your soul blueprint but also the choice to not follow it. You were free to think and do as you please. This luxury was not available on other planets because of the creation of free will. It was unknown how the design of the Great Forgetting would affect souls who incarnated on Earth; hence, it was an experiment.

Because free will was a new creation, many souls queued up chose to experience this new creation. However, due to the density of Earth, and the design to forget, coupled with free will, the souls that came here were sucked into the density. They became stuck and diverted from any soul missions previously set in their blueprint often using their divine gifts which at this time humans were consciously aware for personal gain which in turn started to turn into perversion and self-destruction, their creations were coming from a space of negative intentions rather than pure intentions.

While they were here, these souls lost themselves so much that their actions and creations were having a negative effect on all other life, including in other dimensions. So action was taken by HEB's (higher evolved beings E.Ts) to suspend the knowing of their spiritual heritage and gifts, to avoid complete destruction of earth and humanity. The way this was done was through lowering the vibration of the cosmic field around earth which resulted in the restriction of access to the higher consciousness energy field which surrounded earth previously. This is why Earth and higher civilizations such as Lemuria, mu and Atlantis all suffered catastrophic destruction, it was a part of the plan to hide the sacred wisdom until humanity was soulfully mature enough to understand their heritage and use their gifts for the highest good, so even though souls were seventh-dimensional beings, they dropped back down to third-dimensional and got stuck here. Before they could leave, they had to relearn all they had forgotten and heal all karmic energy, which was created at the time of the misuse of the gifts which had been bestowed onto us.

As you read this, you may be able to relate, or it may bring back your soul understanding.

There were three waves of souls that came here to Earth, each wave slightly upgraded than the one before it not in spiritual wisdom but in soul makeup, in the hope of helping the other lost souls remember their essences and so that they could access their own spiritual understandings and bring healing. But each wave that came also got stuck and ended up the same as the other souls, so there was a call for another lot of souls to help those who had become stuck—the fourth wave, which was the cosmic seeds we have spoken about, the 144,000 light workers that the Bible prophesized. The difference with these being and the ones who came before was that these souls came from many different places across the cosmos, and all held unique gifts to help the lost souls back home. They were extremely upgraded compared to the previous souls who incarnated on Earth. Their bodies were made up slightly differently, and they were and are able to carry more light and retain more spiritual wisdom within their DNA blueprint and light body (aura) than any of the previous souls, which were then activated when the new grids were placed around Earth.

Despite the lowering of energy around the Earth due to the misuse of divine gifts, the fourth wave of souls still held strong seventh-dimensional spiritual understandings and wisdom (and higher in very rare cases) within their DNA. These souls are known as old souls. Through out history these have been civilizations such as the Hopi, Native Americas, Tibetan

Buddhists, as well as many newly born souls upon earth today, as in the late 80's many more old souls started to incarnate on earth. These have been known as star children, indigo children, or rainbow children.

To simplify, the fourth wave of souls is today's old souls and are mainly cosmic seeds. The first wave is today's mature souls going into the old-soul phase. The second wave is the young souls going into the mature-soul phase. Finally, the third wave is the infant souls going into the young-soul phase.

Regardless of what wave your soul might be in—cosmic seed or star seed—each soul group is just as important as the other.

In each soul group, we learn new understandings of the world we perceive and new lessons that promote soul growth and spiritual understandings and ultimately allow us to climb to the next level on the spiritual ladder, bringing us one step closer to discovering our true essence and divine purpose.

This information may be confusing, but be patient with yourself, and you will understand. To make it a little easier, I'll put it like this: Let's say there are five groups of soul advancement, and within the 5 groups there are sub stages 1-7, each sub stage offers a soul a new experiences to form better understandings of its relation to the universe, and its divine nature. For instance a soul in the mature group at sub stage 2 within the 7 sub stages will have a different view on itself and the world round them, for example let's take politics, a soul who is at stage 2 with the mature group it may believe that politics is for the benefit of the humanity and its encompassed communities, whereas by the time the souls elevates to sub stage 7 within the mature soul group, it may find itself not really concerned with the idea of politics full stop, or seeing a whole different perspective of the experience of politics and their agendas. Same can be said with sex for instance.

Another example let's take a soul in the group of an old soul at sub stage 5, now at this point souls at this point are moving away from the idea of sex being just something we do to procreate or to expression affection to one another to a more complex understanding of the power of sexual energy and its effect on the spiritual aspect of its soul and its evolution, yet a soul in the same group but at sub stage 1 may be coming out the idea of celibacy and repression of sexuality.

So, let's look at a quick overview of the soul groups and their current occupancy (estimate) on mother earth. This I hope will give you a better understanding of why we have so much diverse beliefs, lifestyles and concepts, and also why the world is the way that is it right now in regard to the collective views, opinions and beliefs.

Baby: 5% of the population
Infant: 15% of the population
Young: 30% of the population
Mature: 46% of the population
Old: 4% of the population

Where one is will depend on its previous incarnations and the spiritual understanding of itself that it has obtained. By the time a soul has progressed from the baby phase, so to speak, to the old phrase, it will have redeveloped a true understanding of who and what it is, embodying and creating that in the physical and tuning into the higher frequencies. It will become an know itself to be an unlimited source of wisdom, knowledge, spiritual abilities, and understanding of life through healing, meditation, mindfulness, and consciousness manifestation. Therefore, it is the old souls who are the light workers, the bringers of new light and wisdom. They are tuned into angels and spirits, and they are psychic and can access higher spiritual wisdom, whilst always coming from a space of loving intention.

It's only when you hit the old soul phase that you move to a higher understanding and can reconnect at these levels. The rest are just building blocks to get to you to that level of understanding.

There was a time when a lot of mature but mainly young souls were incarnating on Earth. But now, we are in unprecedented times. Earth's energy fields are new and higher than they have ever been, and Earth's position in the cosmos is at a higher vibration than previously. Therefore, a lot of old souls or cosmic seeds are incarnating here, coming to help the lost souls who are starting to remember their Divine essence through new thinking and higher consciousness awareness, music, and spiritual technology. They are coming because of the current state things are in due to collectively created past karmic energy. Also, for a soul who chose a path to become a master of the universe, Earth is the best place for it to create and experience that.

Just because you may be an old soul in this lifetime doesn't mean you have never been a baby soul. All souls go through these stages of soul advancement. The only difference is that some souls chose to progress their spiritual remembrance quicker, meaning a soul may choose lives with more extreme experiences than others, and that is perfectly fine. Every soul is right where it needs to be for its own evolution and remembrance of what and who it truly is.

Souls in the early sub-stages of their particular group may differ in understanding and beliefs from those in the same group but further along and closer to the leap to the next stage. For instance, a young soul at substage two of that soul age group would differ in its beliefs around politics, religion, sex, relationships, the meaning of life, and so on, then that of a young soul at sub stage five. Each stage within a soul's progression brings with it new and higher understandings. The higher the soul age group and sub-stage, the more divine remembrance it will begin to embody.

Soul age is the reason why we can talk about deeper, more far-out theories and ideas to certain people despite age, while others get angry or simply dismisses them. It's the reason for the experiences you're having right now and the reason why you resonate and attract (and get along with) with certain people regardless of Earth age. A soul can only fathom philosophies and ideas which is at its own current level of inner vibratory frequency gained from life and spiritual understandings and experiences obtained not only in its current incarnation but also all its previous incarnations. Regardless of where one may be with its spiritual evolution, we must remember each soul is where it needs to be for its own personal advancement, so let us not judge but elevate and help one another grow. If a soul doesn't understand you or disagrees, that is perfectly fine. We are all heading the same way and cannot fail in our spiritual soul understanding. We are finding our way home to the Great Source, where we all meet up once again.

All stages of a soul's growth and development are essential to its experience. None is grander or greater than the other. But it's only when a soul hits the later stages of the mature phase and heads into the early-old soul phase that it truly starts to understand and embody what and who it truly is here in the physical. That is where you are now. Those reading this book are all in the old-soul or coming into the old-soul phase, whether they are a star seed or cosmic seed—even if you are not consciously aware of it.

Ultimately, everything in the world stems from the Divine Source—consciousness, understanding, and remembering everything is of the same Source, each is at its own level of soul understanding and remembrance. Everything in this world is energy, not this idea of physicality or materialism. Everything is a vibration in a constant state of change and flow, meaning everything is evolving.

Old souls are easy to see and feel, and they stand out from the younger soul ages. They tend to be quite the oddballs, thinking and living in ways that seem alien to others and, in their early days, alien to themselves too. They tend to be into things and believe things that the modern world and its society deem hippy-ish, far-out, or just plain fiction, such as angels, tarot cards, psychics, alternative medicine, the power of intention and imagination, health healing, and crystals, as opposed to the everyday conventions of healing. They talk with more emotional depth rather than social talk of popular culture and media celebrities.

Old souls are those that have broken away from social norms and programming, adopting and creating alternative understandings of the meaning of life and how we all fit into the master plan. Old souls are the ones here at this moment who are being the change they wish to see in the world. They have the courage to step up and stand out and show that there is another way. They are the ones bringing the light and showing the Divine love to illuminate the path home, which, in turn, raises the vibrations of mature souls and even some young souls.

While old souls are predominately the ones showing and creating Divine love in their experiences, mature souls are also reawakening their spiritual understanding and wisdom, having their DNA activated, and having their spiritual understandings brought to the surface.

All souls go through these stages of development and evolution. Just because one is into meditation or metaphysics and understanding soul while others are more interested in the materialistic side of life or pop culture doesn't make any of us better than the others. It is simply because older souls have chosen specially to help earth and humanity in itself collective consciousness evolution, as I said before. In doing so, they chose to develop their spiritual aspect at a quicker pace, to bring about spiritual understandings quicker, normally facing harder life experiences early on.

It's not a race. We are all where we need to be to learn that which the soul is trying to learn or understand about itself. We are all helping one another remember who we truly are and our original missions here on Earth. And we are all heading the same place: back home to the Great Spirit.

The Message about Soul Age

All souls before coming to earth were and must be at a 7th dimensional level of consciousness, as earth is classed as an advanced school for souls compared to other planter systems.

Soul age is simply a reference point to where one is in relation to this divine journey and understanding of spirituality and spiritual concepts.

Earth herself is consciousness and is also growing in her understanding of her essence.

Soul Age has nothing to do with physical age as we know it on earth, and either does being older or younger be better than the other, as we all go through these stages of consciousness evolution.

There are 5 major soul groups baby, infant, mature and old, each have substages 1-7, a soul understanding and ability to embody higher vibratory concepts will depend on its current soul group and substage.

Many souls have come to earth and have got stuck due to the density of the vibration on earth, and due to misuse of knowledge in the earlier days which we are still recovering and healing from. Due to many souls becoming stuck actions were put in place to help those souls to come back to their original spiritual consciousness state, this is what is referred to as clarion call.

We are all moving through the spiritual hierarchy, and all is going to come to same spiritual understandings and conclusions as we elevate own inner vibratory frequency, moving us closer to that of the frequency of God or Great Spirit.

Soul age is how far along a soul is within its spiritual development and evolution. We are all going through the same stages of remembrance by design. No matter where each soul is, it is right where it needs to be. We are all finding our way back home to Great Source and doing so by being and expressing the qualities of Divine love/God/Great Spirit.

Soul wants you to remember that soul is the reason for the people you attract, people who on the same soul age vibratory frequency will be attracted to the each other.

Understandings, characteristics and personality all depends on one's soul age. Different soul ages perceive situations and subjects differently.

Even soul within the same soul group can dramatically differ in philosophies, morals and ideals.

The Soul Plan and Soul Lessons

As discussed in the previous chapter, we are all at different stages of our remembrance and soul development. None is better than the other, and all are right where they need to be concerning where they are within their journeys of remembrance. So, what is a soul plan and what are soul lessons?

Before a soul incarnates or reincarnates, it creates a plan or blueprint based on what it has learned and remembered about who and what it is from experience obtained in its previous lives, and also from what other negative karmic energy it may have accidently created. The soul then uses this blueprint as a reference point for where it is in its understanding or remembrance or, simply put, where it is in its spiritual journey and what it wishes to experience, and heal in its next lifetime so that it can become closer to the mind and essence of God.

Ultimately, soul lessons are created so that we can experience certain energies which gives soul the opportunity to manifest and express its true divine nature, all experiences are created to lead us to experience the heart energy and the remembrance of our essence, to ultimately align with the souls divine nature on the physical plane.

We get together with our angels and guides, as well as other souls, and put together a plan of experiences solely for this purpose. In this basic plan, we agree to major events that we may experience (be it good or bad).

By major I mean experiences such as the relationships we may experience and with whom, any physical or mental disabilities we may be faced with, the jobs we get, the friends we have, and the family in which we chose to incarnate into, all to help us on our soul and spiritual journeys. It is often easy to identify major life lessons because the chosen outcomes of that experiences produce drastic change in one's self and one's physical experience and affect more than your single soul.

The soul chooses any major life-changing experiences before it comes here, along with those who are involved in that experience, and all who have that experience have chosen to have that experience. Yes, even those we label enemies and villains came to us and, out of pure Divine love, agreed to be a part of the experience so that they, too, can grow and develop. This arrangement can be called a soul contract.

This is where the age-old debate of predestination vs free will comes in. It's often argued that if we have free will then how is it there are predestined events waiting for us. I struggled to understand this for a while until one day in my mediation my guide gave me this explanation. As I mentioned earlier soul chooses certain energies it wishes to experience in the physical, these energies show up as physical situations or events (physical manifestation of the chosen energy) now to soul it just wants you to see all situations from the perspective of higher self, being that of love compassion, forgiveness joy and understanding, but when on the physical plan it is not as straight forward as that, although we have a predestined event created for us, we don't have a predestined outcome. This is where free will comes into play. Soul may choose the major life lesson and have an idea of what it wishes the outcome to be, but when on the physical plane as a free will manifestation of Great Spirit we are given the choice, we chose how we perceive the lesson, and ultimately the outcome of this lesson.

The more aligned with your soul and higher self you are the more the outcome will be that of what soul had previous hoped to achieve and thus passes it without creation of additional negative karmic energy, but it has often been the case that souls when in physical, do not see the lesson or experience for what it truly is, and thus from this distorted perspective creates outcomes which wasn't necessarily the desired outcome for soul. This is where principle of uncertainty comes in play. Due to the fact that time is not liner but all happening at once, meaning that all outcomes are being played out at once, it is up to the soul in the physical as to what comes from each lesson, a person may choose to see the lesson from the original perspective of soul straight away but due to having to do inner work, as well as train one's self to reconnect with their true essence (higher self) this is often not the case, well not in the first instance. Often because of the heavy program of fear, souls do not see the lesson for what it is, and create outcomes which aren't necessarily in alignment with its goal, these outcomes produce negative karmic energy signatures which then will be repeatedly created until it is healed by soul, this is how negative karmic energy is created, if the energy is not healed in the lifetime it was created it through love understanding and forgiveness, it will be chosen in the next life as major life lessons by soul which will then be made manifest in the souls next physical incarnation until it is seen for what it was and healed.

All negative karmic energy is a created by soul by coming from the energy of fear and doubt rather than love and faith when perceiving its life lessons and human experience.

Although the soul chooses and creates its soul plan and what it wishes to experience in its next lifetime, it cannot predict 100% of the experiences, energies, or lessons it may face. There may be some experiences that the soul didn't create within its plan because they were created unconsciously on the physical plane. As unconscious creations then produce their own energy signatures which in turn create corresponding experiences that match the signature. Again, the only way to cease creation of these unconscious creations is to heal the experience with the energy of forgiveness and love through meditation and visualization.

This may be confusing to you, so let's make it clearer.

Let's say your soul in its soul blueprint created an energy which produces an experience of an abusive relationship in the physical with the hoped outcome that you will realize your self-worth, strength and ability to stand on your own two feet, the goal of soul is for you to break away from this abusive relationship, to stand on your own two feet and support yourself whilst forgiving the other person, after all this soul agreed out of divine love with you to have this experience so you could express these qualities, and see this experience from the energy of love, but whilst acting out this experience in the physical you come from an energy of fear and doubt, so you stay in the relationship until you can't accept the situation no more, finally you break away, but rather than forgiving the other person you curse and blame the other for the experience, the feelings and emotions you had experience, and hold on to these thoughts of hate and resentment. The holding on to these negative thoughts and feelings then create a new outcome which wasn't necessarily in alignment with what soul wanted to achieve, this chosen outcome coming from the energy of resentment and hate then created negative karmic energy. This newly created energy of hate and resentment brings forth experiences which match the energy signature of hate and resentment in order for this energy to healed. For example, you may find yourself in repeated situations or experiences where by the feelings of hate and resentment arise, maybe a friend stole from you, maybe someone had been talking badly about you, this has manifested because now before you can climb up the ladder of soul evolution you must heal that karmic energy of hate and resentment to move back into the energy of divine love. Before any soul can grow in itself evolution it must heal all negative karma. So, whilst the original goal of soul was for you to experience abuse as a means to realize your true inner strength, you have now accidently or unconsciously created an energy of hate and resentment. Yet if you in the first instance was able to perceive the experience of abuse for its original intention that being of love to show to you your inner ability of strength and courage, and the love of the other (the abuser) through forgiveness and compassion you would not have created the experience of a friend stealing from you, or someone talking badly about you, because you hadn't created the energy of hate and resentment in the first instance.

So, you see yes there are predestined events for us, and a desired outcome for soul, but no there is not a predestined outcome, that is chosen by us.

Just know that although you have free will of choice, the major life lessons soul agreed to in its blueprint will continuously manifest on the physical plane until the soul on the physical plane aligns with the soul's desired outcome chosen on the spirit plane.

Major life lessons will continually show up until you see from the eyes of divine love, and act from the perspective of the higher soul.

A soul can also decide to change its soul plan mid-way in the human experience, again this is not always the case, but it does happen, often because soul has stayed so far from its desired path.

The Divine Order

This is a perfect moment to mention Divine timing or Divine order, which basically means that certain people, events, and experiences that were agreed upon in your soul plan will only come around at the perfect time and not before. Remember, *the Great Spirit is never late*. That's why great masters such as Buddha, Jesus, Yeshua all remind us to be patient and trust the Great Source, basically reminding us that there is a plan, and if something is meant to be, it will be. No matter how much you force it or want it, it will only come to you when the timing is divinely perfect in relation to your soul plan and your soul development. The more we want something to happen or want to hold on to something, the more we are showing a lack of trust in the Divine flow, abundance, and timing of the Universe. The chances are that the wanting or longing for that thing or person will only cause you to never have that person or thing.

From the limited third-dimension perspective, it may seem as if these events or encounters are just random, but as all masters have told us for eons, nothing is random. We always get what we ask for and, in fact, co-created with the Great Source. In hard times when we feel stress or depression, there is a plan. Those mental states are merely a lack of understanding of who and what we are. When we truly remember this fact, we can transmute the feelings of stress, depression, and anxiety. We come to remember that those mental states are states created by focusing on fear-based experiences or outcomes and are just experiences created by illusions.

Even those situations we label as "a problem" serve to promote soul growth, coming out stronger and wiser in the end. You only have to look at how far you have come, from who you thought you were to who you are now and, ultimately, to what you wish to be and create in your next grandest moment.

When you tune in to the higher energies, raise your vibration, and start to rediscover who you truly are, your soul will shine forth. You will become aware of your purpose, and that is when you can bring and create your heaven on this Earth.

The Message about the Soul Plan and Soul Lessons

The soul plan is created before incarnating on earth.
It is created with your angel's guides and other soul who have agreed to co-created certain experiences together.

Nothing in life is random. For each person and situation, there is a greater reason, a greater picture that the soul sees. You are here to remember who you truly are, which is done

41

through experiences so we can emotionally express our inner divine nature. No matter how they are perceived, one's personal experience are part of the soul blueprint, have been agreed upon, and are in place for you to remember the love you made from and the love you wish to express or be. Whether they are big or small, all lessons (energies of remembrance) present us with a beautiful opportunity to ascend the ego and rise into the heart.

Soul lessons are created by the soul to simply promote remembrance of its divine heritage in the physical.

No lessons or experiences are against us, that includes those experiences which are not perceived to be "good" or "pleasant" this is because to soul all experiences bring with its potential soul growth and evolution.

Soul Contracts

What is a soul contract? A soul contract is basically a pre-agreement between souls upon one's soul tree, to come into this life and co-create certain experiences we have asked for in order to grow our understanding of our divine heritage. These experiences can come in the form of a relationship, job, friends, and family. That is what our essence and life are all about—helping and encouraging our individual and collective soul growth here in the physical.

A soul tree is a term used to define the group of souls in which you choose to incarnate with, often many times playing different roles in each, for instance in one life time your current parents could have been your children, or your best friend in this life, your sibling in a previous life. It's often quite easy to identify souls which are a part of your soul tree by the recognition on a soul level. Maybe you meet someone who you feel like you've known for years, maybe as a child you parent your parents, meaning you act like your parents are your children. Souls on your soul tree are often called "soul family"

Your soul tree consists of your parents, family, friends, work colleagues and pets, anyone who plays a role in your life experience is a part of your soul tree. The reason for the soul to incarnate into certain soul trees vary. Only the soul itself knows the reason for choosing its current soul tree. Often reasons are because there has been karmic energy created between one or more souls upon the soul tree which need to be healed, or maybe a group of souls have agreed to come together to create a certain experience, or to preform group soul healing through a group physical experience.

Soul will always choose a soul tree which offers what it needs to grow in itself development and understanding of divine heritage and wisdom. This offering may be to be healed, to offer healing, to elevate other members of your soul tree in understanding of divine wisdom and God given gifts, or simply because your soul enjoys the presence and resonate of your current soul tree members.

You are not bound to one soul tree it's always a choice, often soul will jump from one soul tree to next as it grows in itself awareness of its divine nature, but before it can do this it must heal any karmic energy that has been created within its current soul tree members.

There is much information on soul tree's available so if you resonate with this then go ahead and do your own research, you may just uncover so hidden truths you haven't been aware of.

Before we incarnate or reincarnate, we come together in the spirit plane in a pure spirit state and call out for certain experiences in which certain souls will answer and come to us. They will agree that they will appear at certain points in our human experience to give us that experience or healing. All souls involved will benefit, grow, and expand their soul perspective.

No soul comes to us or us to them unless we choose or ask either so we can heal or learn from them or vice versa, or as I like to put it, give an experience that promotes acts of remembrance of who we truly are or who they truly are. This includes those experiences labeled "bad" or "traumatic." As discussed earlier, there is nothing soul sees as bad and nothing

it sees as wrong in the spirit world. These labels and judgments were created out fear here in the third dimension by us and those who wish to keep us from ascending and, ultimately, prevent us from remembering who we are and what we are doing here.

We must remember that we choose and co-create everything in our human experience whether it be conscious or unconscious, including our fathers and mothers, partners, pregnancies, marriages, life milestones, travels, moves abroad, careers, and social circles. Even experiences such as abusive relationships, rape, murder, and so forth are agreements made in our contracts because all souls grow from those experiences.

I have found that when it comes to "bad experiences," the main lessons we all learn are forgiveness, understanding, and compassion. Only when we forgive can we release, heal, and move forward. That is also the main reason why we have karma and attachments to souls who we don't resonate with on the physical plane. However, only the soul or souls involved in the experience will know its reason for calling out for and creating this experience. Just remember that even those who gave you "bad" experiences came to you out of Divine love when you called on the spirit to have this experience. You signed that soul contract together in pure Divine love.

Many philosophers, religious leaders, and ascended masters have said, "Let us not judge." Why? Because we don't know about the contracts agreed upon, what the soul's life lessons are, or what that soul is trying to learn or remember about itself.

The main reason we feel it's okay to judge others is that we have been taught that God judges us, so we take on that idea ourselves. But despite what organized religion says, not even the Great Spirit judges you, and it never will. This idea is a distortion to create a separation between you and the Great Spirit. The Great Spirit does not and will not forsake you.

All experiences will remain and repeat until we all learn and see the experiences and lessons for what they are. There's a saying that goes, "What you resist persists. What you see disappears." It's only when we see all through the eyes of love, the essence of the Great Spirit, and ourselves that our eyes will be truly open, and only then will we be free of the chains of illusion and separation.

The Message about Soul Contracts

Soul contracts are made with souls who are on your current soul tree.

Once you have healed or gained what you can from your soul tree you will jump and move to others.

Each soul tree offers new knowledge and experience, as well as opportunity to either grow in or share divine understandings.

All souls before coming to earth create a soul contract with many beings. Contracts can be made with no just other human beings but also angels and ETs.

Nothing a soul experiences is against it, all experiences are beneficial for its evolution, this includes those people we class as enemies and those experiences we judge as "bad"

Contracts can last more than just one lifetime; in many cases they last for many years.

As a soul goes through itself earth experience it can change it agreements, it can choose to terminate one due to gaining and giving it all it can to that soul, and also create new ones.

Soul contracts will last as long as it takes for the soul(s) to gain what it needs from the experiences it has.

The main reason for soul contracts is to elevate one another is our spiritual remembrance often through experiences of nonjudgmental understandings, forgiveness and love.

Souls are a part of a soul tree in which more often than not contains the people you will meet in your human experience. However, once a soul feels it has been giving and gave all it can from those souls it can chose to jump to a new soul tree, which will bring new people and experiences into the human experience.

A Soul may experience role reversals in different life times, meaning your child could have been your mother in a previous life, or your mother from a previous life is your child in this lifetime.

Family and Friends

Despite how we perceive in the physical, we affect the lives of most people we interact with, or they affect ours as soul tree members as spoken about in the previous chapter.

There is far much more going on with soul, its journey, and the complexity of the plan than we can fathom or understand at this current vibrational level, so don't worry if you don't have all answers to things mentioned here and throughout this book, it all comes in perfect divine timing.

In this chapter, we'll discuss family and friends. We'll look at why some souls reincarnate into what would be deemed socially successful and accepting family, why others to choose harsher conditions and life experiences, why some souls choose an "easy life" full of love and joy, and why others choose a "not-so-easy life" full of fear and worry. Again, none of this is random or a coincidence but all part of our choosing and soul plan.

Everyone that touches our lives is a blessing to us. Before leaving the spirit, plane and coming to Earth, we choose and know who our family will be—our mothers and fathers, our brothers and sisters. Even if we don't know it when in the physical, all souls have an understanding on the soul level of the experiences we as a family they will have.

One question I used to ask myself and that a lot of people ask me is if we choose our life experiences, why we choose an environment full of negativity, violence, and a lack of love? Why would you chosen parents who don't show love? You must remember that to be that which you are, you must experience that which you are not. This concept may be a little confusing,

so, let me put it like this: Let's say we conceptionally know ourselves to be Divine love on the spirit plane. The soul wants to feel, experience, and be the love it conceptionally knows itself to be in spirit by creating it in the physical. When the soul experiences it, creates it, and becomes it in the physical, it is complete in that certain experience and can it tick if off its list, so to speak.

To do so this most effectively, the soul may choose an experience in which there is a lack of Divine love. The soul could choose an experience of more Divine love, but it's only through an experience of what might seem like a lack of Divine love that the soul can express and create itself to its fullest. By putting itself in an experience that lacks Divine love, it creates a Divine opportunity to bring forth balance and create more Divine love.

For the soul to know that which it is, it must experience that which it is not. This experience can be called a reference point for the soul. If the soul chose an experience of pure Divine love, it wouldn't be able to know itself in the physical as pure Divine love. It would not need to create or express that aspect of itself because Divine love is already present in this Earthly experience, thereby not promoting much soul growth and remembrance.

Let's put it another way. Let's say we have two circles—a white circle and a black circle— and a grey dot. The white circle is life space filled with Divine love, the black circle is life space with no Divine love, and the grey dot is the soul (Figure below).

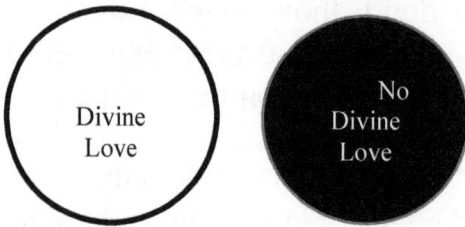

Figure 1. Life space filled with Divine love, life space with no Divine love, and the soul

The soul wants to create its soul understanding of Divine love and its feeling in the physical. It could choose to live in the white circle, but it wouldn't experience any growth because it wants to create the experience by itself, not be born into it. Therefore, it is more likely to choose to live in the black circle so it can create and experience Divine love fully by expanding itself and turning the black circle white with its own understanding and creation (Figure 2).

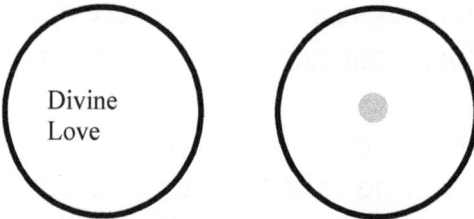

Figure 2. Life space with no Divine love (right) transformed by the soul

That is what all of our souls are doing, and why it may choose what seems to us to be a hard life or life lacking something. We're all here to make the black circle white, turning that lack of something into more of something, How? By remembering who we truly are and creating and expressing that in the physical. We use our Divine tools to turn that circle from black to white.

Whether the soul is having what may seem to us in the physical as easy human experiences or hard human experiences, both offer the soul needed experience to promote itself soul growth, and neither is no better than the other. No matter where a soul is in its journey or what it is being, it is at the perfect place for its soul understanding and remembrance.

Who knows what previous life a soul chose? It's quite possible that those who seem to have it all made for them in this life had it "hard" in a previous life and had a tougher life experience. Similarly, those souls that choose a tougher human experience in this life may have chosen an easier life experience previously. It's all about balance.

Many factors are considered when a soul chooses a family to be born into and the groups of friends it gains, but it ultimately depends on where a soul is in its spiritual journey and its soul tree. You may incarnate with souls you have incarnated with in a previous life or lives, and those souls tend to be members of your soul tree. You all may just love to be around one another's energy or have a lot to teach one another. Or it could be that you created past karma with these souls in previous lives, so you have come into this life to heal through forgiveness and letting go, releasing that karmic energy, so to speak, from growing in the understanding of who you truly are and what you're here to do.

You may decide to reincarnate into a family that seems to be on a different level or have a vibration from yours. In these instances, those souls may have asked you to join their soul tree to elevate there soul growth and spiritual understanding, or you may have asked to join so that you can bring in your spiritual gifts to practice healing. Either way, no matter what family, friend, or enemy experience a soul has, it chooses that experience and will gain perfectly in terms of soul understanding from its created experience.

Much can be said about our friends—again, factors such as soul tree, karma, and soul contracts are considered.

As you go through life, experiences change your vibrations. It's a part of the cosmic flow of life—that ebb and flow I mentioned at the beginning of this book.

You may find that the friends you were once really close to will fade away, and new people who you resonate with will appear. This change is simply because you have learned what we need to from one another, and your vibrations (paths) require different experiences to grow. When a soul gets to this point, it goes its own way. Not all paths that our friends and we take will end up that way. Souls can and do chose to be connected for life—that school friend or work colleague you stay connected with even when you leave that school or workplace.

It's really up to those souls involved in the experience. But ultimately, if that friend or enemy doesn't support your vibration and Divine path, then they will go their own way, and you will go your way, and that is perfectly okay.

The reason I have explained the above is to help bring clarity to why a soul would chose parents who don't show their child love, or why a soul would choose what seems like an experience of poverty, or friends which don't support you.

It can be difficult in the physical when trying to understand the reason for external circumstances, just remember that everything is for you, and not against you, it is for the benefit of your soul's growth even if you don't see it now, in time and with experience you will.

If you find that you experience a lack of in any area of your life be it love, excitement, adventure and joy ask yourself why? What is the reason for your being where you are at in that moment? What opportunity does your external experience offer you? Ask these questions and you will start to fully understand why you chose such parents, why you have the friends you do.

The Message about Family and Friends

Our friends and family are not just random, they are often a part of our current soul tree. They serve to help us and us them to remember who you and they truly are.

We reincarnate with the same souls from our soul tree many times, often playing new roles, for instance you could have been the brother of your now best friend, or you could have been the mother of your current earthly mother.

We chose our family's and are aware of the energy and experience those parents and family's will bring, for soul it has nothing to do with blood but simply chosen growth.

A soul may choose what may be perceived as a negative experience in order allow itself to create the positive within the negative. As mentioned in the "Lack of" diagram.

Once a lesson or soul contract is complete, we create a new experience with new family and friends and again the wheel turns.

Soul wants to feel and physically create in the physical what it knows itself to be, in most cases in order to do this it will place itself in an experience whereby there is a lack of that energy, simply because that's where best it can see its results of the intended creation in the physical.

As we grow in our divine remembrance and evolve, we jump from soul tree to soul tree each bringing with it new souls who may be your family members or friends in the next life.

Love and Relationships

Everything I have mentioned in this book so far boils down to the remembrance of the Divine love that we are and that created us and the way we perceive ourselves, the Universe, and our relation to it. To create a new, clearer understanding of the real nature of love, we are going to need to redefine what we believe love to be, but let's quickly summarize the idea of beliefs.

Throughout our lives, we collect facts through observation and experience as proof that regulate our beliefs. These facts then become deeply established in our subconscious. Through repetitive patterns of thinking and holding onto the same notion, we eventually transform opinions into beliefs.

In the beginning beliefs are flexible, but over time as we come more ingrained into the physical realm, they become fixed and inflexible. Finally, we reach a point at which beliefs become so strong that, despite repeated evidence to the contrary, we are no longer willing to consider a fresh perspective.

To know if a belief is really your own or preprogrammed, simply ask yourself, "How does this belief make me feel not just emotionally but physically as well?" Beliefs and ideas that come from your essence will give you a good feeling, causing a rise in energy within the body, forcing a smile, and so on (always take note of the physical feelings). Beliefs that have been programmed on an inner level and that you don't agree with tend to come with some inner conflict and tightening around the solar plexus. It's as if your soul knows that you are holding onto a value that has been forced or programmed, holding onto a moral value that isn't yours, and when you truly ask yourself about it, you seldom agree with it. The greater your beliefs line up with what you want, and who you think you are, the grander your reality will be.

In the third dimension, we have all been taught unconsciously that love is conditional, meaning that we only give it if we get something in return. As with most things in life, we have turned love into a trade. We say, "Yeah, I love you, but if you don't live up to these conditions and agreements, then I won't love you anymore." This idea is one of the biggest distortions in the world today. This lack of love is a major factor contributing to the state of the world today.

Divine love is unconditional. The love the Great Spirit has for us all is unconditional. Therefore, the love we have for ourselves and others should be unconditional as well. Instead, we have turned this pure, beautiful energy and experience into one of conditions and trades. Yes, we trade our love. There's a saying here on earth that "nothing comes for free," which exactly what has been created.

We have turned love into something to trade, almost saying, "I'll meet her needs if she meets mine." This mindset causes major issues. We find ourselves constantly trying to figure out what others want, forgetting what we want and, more so, the Divine purpose of holy relationships.

We have been programmed to conditionally love not only our fellow human beings but also ourselves. We have been taught that we can only love ourselves if we have never done anything "wrong," or if we have lived up to the standards set by religion. Because of this distortion, we have seen an increase in souls that experience a lack of love for themselves, in turn creating or attracting mainly unloving, fearful experiences and feelings of depression and anxiety as the reason why they might attract unloving relationships.

To get a full understanding, we need to trace our beliefs about love back to the beginning. They stem from mainstream and religion. Yes, whether you're aware of it or not, your core believes and morals are derived from not only your teachers, parents, and siblings but also good old organized religion and are the very laws and morals that govern society and most of the world. These laws have been known as the "Commandments," and they appear across all religions. The only real laws of the laws of the universe which I will discuss later on.

The Commandments were not meant to be commands as God/Great Spirit commands nothing of you, it was a misinterpretation of the ancient message purposely given to the collective, also there are groups that want you to live in fear of these ideals because they benefit consciously and financially by creating mass fear and judgement by creating this idea you will go to a place called Hell if you don't follow these guidelines and repent your sins in a so called house of God (church).

These commandments are guidelines rather than commands on how to live in a higher vibrational state of peace and harmony both individually and collectively by encouragement of coming from the heart space and love rather than headspace and ego/fear, resulting in the expansion of our consciousness. By understanding that directive and following these guidelines freely, you will also be prevented from creating matching negative energy karma and, thus, repetitive negative cycles in your human experience, making way for more positive and higher vibrational experiences to be manifested.

This distortion and the idea that the Great Spirit judges people based on the Commandments brought upon Earth and its people by those who wish to control them is also part of the reason why there is so much war. It is the reason why we have separated ourselves from ourselves, others, and the universe and why people are dying from obesity on one side of the while millions die of starvation on the other. It is the reason why we have separated ourselves from the Great Spirit, our angels, and the Divine Universe. It is the reason why churches and corporations have gained such power and influence in the doings of the world. It is the reason why we think so little of ourselves and one another. It is the reason why we have handed over our power to corporations and businesses that don't care about their people or the world but only the size of their profits. It is the reason why we fear death, which in turn stops us from truly living. It is the reason why we model ourselves and our beliefs on what media tells us to think and believe. It is the reason why we have allowed those in power to form our collective opinions through so-called entertainment and media propaganda.

The Great Spirit doesn't judge you or care what you do. It simply cares (a little) what you chose to be in that moment. It really doesn't care if you chose not to follow the guidelines—it will not curse you or stop loving you—because it knows that through enough experiences, you will come to understand exactly what these guidelines mean, the Divine purpose they were given to us for, and most importantly, who you truly are.

It wise to know that by the term "guidelines," we are referring to the guidelines that have been given to us so that we can create a life of heaven—bring a personal experience of heaven to Earth which in turn helps to bring a collective experience of heaven on earth—without creating repetitive negative karmic patterns and, thus, bringing negative experiences upon yourself.

Let's remind ourselves of these guidelines:

1. You shall have no other gods before me.
2. You shall not make for yourself an idol in the form of anything.
3. You shall not misuse the name of the Lord your God.
4. Remember the Sabbath day by keeping it holy.
5. Honor your father and your mother.
6. You shall not murder.

7. You shall not commit adultery.
8. You shall not steal.
9. You shall not give false testimony against your neighbor.
10. You shall not covet your neighbor's house, wife, or property.

Looking at this list, you can start to see where society's morals are derived from.

It's not the Commandments as such that have caused such separation but the idea that we are born in sin and that the Great Spirit judges us because of this, resulting in us being sent to the burning pits of hell but only if we don't mold our lives according to the commands given, which is yet another distortion. Because of this false belief and pre-programming brought upon us by organized religion, we have taken this idea that God judges good and bad and placed it on ourselves, seeing ourselves as the righteous and pointing the finger at those who differ from ourselves: those who have different beliefs, different backgrounds, and different histories. This finger-pointing has ultimately lead to us placing ourselves in our own versions of hell, living in fear, handing over our power to the corporations, and allowing external influences to create our individual and collective opinions and beliefs to keep us unknowingly chained by our consciousness.

Always remember that the Great Spirit cannot and will not ever infringe on your free will.

Let us first rectify these "commands" and bring more understanding and light to them. If you are deeply religious, then this next section might confuse you, but be patient with yourself. The way to truly get a full understanding of this information is to think of God as I do—as a pure, loving, infinite energy of intelligence that creates and experiences through us and with us, making us, in a sense, God. It has no fear, doesn't judge, and isn't out to get us. It simply wants the total best for our highest good Divine journey, which again, is purely about remembering who we are through various experiences and remembering that we are infinite souls having human experiences, and not that we are humans with a soul. Now with that in mind, let's break some of these so-called Commandments down.

The directive "You shall have no other God before me" is, again, not a command but a piece of advice. Just ask yourself, "What would Divine love make of this?" The Great Source doesn't care who or what you call it or who you worship. It simply loves you and wants only the grandest joy and human experience for you. But it also wants you to be cautious because there have been and still are those who wish to distort the Great Source and your connection to it. They try to distort your connection so that they can control you and that you will pay them for it.

Yes, organized religion is one of the wealthiest sectors here on Earth. They tell you that you must do this and that, do not do this and that, and pay this to get that when it's all a distortion and lies, The Great Spirit does not and will never want your material goods or your money. After all, even those things we label as hard, physical objects are just vibrating particles. The Great Spirit doesn't want you to be controlled or told what to do. It wants you to remember who you are through creation and experience and, thus, reminding those lives you touch of who they truly are. This is called the stone and ripple effect, which we'll talk more about it later.

Let's look at this one next: "You shall not use the Lord's name in vain." Remember, the Great Spirit doesn't judge. It only loves and wants the best for your soul and life experience.

The idea that "you shall not use the Lord's name in vain" contradicts the message of Great Spirit, full stop. "In vain" means "without success or a result." The Great Spirit doesn't judge and doesn't see success in the way we do. The angels and the Great Spirit only see's the truly divine light you are, no matter what you have done, said, or been. It loves you unconditionally and always will. Remember that conditional love was created by humankind. The Great Spirit only sees your growth and, thus, your constant success in your personal life experience, even if you don't.

You will never use the Lord's name "in vain" because there are no lords. You are it. Every experience, situation, and relationship are successful. We gain and grow from them all— yes, even those we call "bad."

What is truly meant by "you shall not use the Lord's name in vain" is that it's not wise to use the Great Spirit to wish negative things upon someone. Asking for harm to come to someone is not wise because, due to the law of free will, you can't do anything to anyone without their permission, and certainly not inflict harm on anyone. Ultimately, whatever you wish upon others comes back at you, be it good or bad. Use your words wisely.

I'm not saying to go out and go against these guidelines. By doing so, you will only create the same outcome upon yourself—that is why we were given them in the first place—so I'm not advocating going out and stealing or taking a person's life. I'm simply saying that it's time to send forgiveness to yourself and others.

Living a life not following these divine guidelines does not make anyone a "bad" soul. As I have repeatedly said, anyone who has had or is having "bad" experiences has asked for them (maybe not on the conscious physical but on a soul, subconsciousness level) so that they can grow their soul understanding and remembrance to a deeper level of the Divine Love we are all, which will ultimately give them a bigger perspective of where they came from and what they are. Don't judge yourself or others but simply show love and compassion, no matter what you may have done in the past. Everything was sent here as a pre-sent gift from your higher self and the Great

Spirit so that you can grow and evolve on a soul level and overcome your chosen life lessons.

As you ascend up the spiritual ladder through multiple incarnations and start to remember who you truly are, you will begin to move out of the lower vibrations of ego and fear gradually climb up to the higher vibrations of Divine love and harmony. You will come to the understanding that there is no good or bad, no right or wrong, and no judgments but only unconditional love and forgiveness for everyone and everything—including you.

When you're coming from a place of Divine love, the Divine guidelines or Commandments will naturally resonate with your being. With all fear aside, the Commandments are guidelines for how to not only live in love and harmony with yourself, others, and the world but also prevent these things from happening to you. We all have the freedom of choice and the free will to choose who we believe we are and wish to be and what we wish to create in relation to the current experience or situation.

Let's look at another commandment—again, coming from a space of Divine love, understanding, and no judgment.

"You shall not steal" really means that you shall never feel the *need* to steal. When you ascend and realize more and more who you truly are and who you wish to create, you will begin to understand that stealing comes from the idea that there isn't enough or that or you can't have something. You will become aware that these ideologies were purposely created from fear and false programming to control our consciousness.

When we are awakened to who we truly are, we will not need to steal. Instead, we will create our wealth and abundance through a combination of utilizing the Divine creative gifts we each have and the practice of visualizing and feeling through mediation or daydreaming—as the saying goes, a belief made manifest. It's also important to know that when we speak of wealth and abundance, we don't just mean monetary wealth but wealth and abundance of health, spiritual wisdom, and much more.

It is not only the Commandments that have caused the illusion of separation. As I briefly mentioned earlier, it's also the idea that we can "sin" or that we are born into "sin." This idea
couldn't be further from the Divine truth. Over time all this distortion and fear-based propaganda have created the world we see today and the programming that has created the way we perceive ourselves and others. Despite what religion, media, and teachers say, there are no sins, and there are no victims nor villains.

Let's go back to some earlier points and circle back around so that you can get a clearer picture of what this all means.

Let's say you're a new soul, just beginning your new Earthly incarnation. You are, in a sense, a baby soul on Earth. You haven't experienced much of the physical world of polarity and duality or separation, so in a sense, you are working your way from the bottom to the top of the soul ages (journey) and back home to the Divine Source. To do so, you must have certain experiences of all extremes, both "good" and "bad." Only when you experience the two ends of the spectrum can you find and understand the equilibrium, creating it in the physical realm through a higher vibrational understanding in the heart of peace, unity, and harmony.

If the idea of "sins" were true, then we would not progress as soulful beings. Every time we grew through having low vibrational experiences, we would be judged and sent to hell, never progressing, and making the experiences pointless because the soul would never progress. However, that is not the case.

Life on Earth is an experience of separation and duality. For something to exist, its opposite must also. Together, the two polar-opposite ends of the spectrum make the whole experience, and there cannot be one without the other. It's the same with our personal experiences.

Let's use love as an example. As I mentioned in the chapter "Life and Its Meaning," for a soul to understand an experience fully, it must experience both extremes of that experience—the "good" and the "bad"—because there cannot be one without the other. Just like with everything else, we have separate spectrums of experiences.

This distortion and lack of understanding is a part of the reason why we find ourselves going around in circles. We label things as "good" or "bad," which causes us to miss the whole reason why the soul created that experience. When we start to understand that there is no "good" or "bad," then we stop judging and can see things for that they truly are rather than what we are told they are.

When you understand this concept—that there is no "good" or "bad"—you will see that even the so-called sins bring amazing opportunities for spiritual growth and development, which is why they are not sins. Every single one of us has and still does commit actions of so-called sins—well, according to what organized religion says—but this observation is merely one from a sense of ego and meant to bring fear upon us so that we might do as we are told. We must experience the lower end of the emotional spectrum to know the counter opposite. After all, let's not forget they are of the same experience except but at different degrees on the scale. We must know and feel the two ends of the emotional spectrum to get to the middle ground (the law of duality or polarity)

To see these sin statements in true Divine light, take away the judgment and fear that the Great Spirit is going to judge you and forsake you. Instead, ask, "What does Divine love make of this statement?"

Let's start with envy. Envy is the painful or resentful awareness of an advantage enjoyed by another joined with a desire to possess the same advantage: "Therefore, rid yourselves of all malice and all deceit, hypocrisy, envy, and slander of every kind. Like newborn babies, crave pure spiritual milk, so that by it you may grow up in your salvation."[1] 1 Peter-2:2

First, let's change the definition of "envy" to what it truly means. Envy doesn't mean wanting something from someone so you can have it instead of them; rather, it means being inspired by someone.to create a similar experience. It means to look up too or to be inspired by, not that you want to take something the other so that they don't have it, but to have what they have without taking away your neighbors. It is not and never will be another form of jealousy in the eyes of the Great Spirit.

With this new definition in mind, you can see that it's not bad or a "sin" to be envious but inspiring. This emotion brings with it the positive experience of emotion and is a great cause of soul growth and development. All you need but do is ask, "What does Divine love make of this feeling or this statement?" or "What does my heart tell me about what I am reading or what I am being told?" The heart is your true brain.

Let's look at one more. Laziness means disinclined to activity or exertion, not energetic or vigorous: "The way of the sluggard is blocked with thorns, but the path of the upright is a highway."[2] I find it hard to believe that laziness was ever a sin or that it even exists. Lifetimes on Earth are trying at the best of times due to the density. In many instances, a soul needs to re-center or reassess a situation, and it may very well want to have a rest or be "lazy."
It is in times of restfulness that the answer to the questions we are asking arise.

Laziness is a label that cannot be defined. How can anyone be called lazy? We don't f what that soul is achieving. We here

---

[1]. 1 Peter 2:1–2.
[2]. Proverbs 15:19.

on Earth often believe that we have to be seen as "doing" things to grow or be successful, but what we have forgotten is that while we may sleep, the soul never does. From a third-person perspective, it may seem as though someone is doing nothing but being "lazy" by not working a regular job, taking regular naps, and not striving in life. But on a soul level, that person might be doing their divine work in the realm of the All while they are sleeping, or they may be going with their intuition and not rushing into finding a job, a house, a partner, etc., just allowing themselves to flow.

As I discussed earlier, everything arrives in perfect Divine timing. On Earth, it could take a day, a week, a year, or many years for something to happen. Just know and speak, "The Infinite Spirit is never late." Just because we perceive someone as doing nothing, it doesn't mean they *are* doing nothing. A lot is going on subconsciously, and no one knows what that may be other than the soul itself.

Who is anyone to judge what is "lazy" and who's is being "lazy"? What is lazy to one person could be perceived as a respite for another. It's all a matter perspective gained through experience, and we all at different stages of experience, remembrance of who we truly are, and the integration of that into the physical. If you need to take a break or be "lazy," go ahead. When the soul has had enough of that experience, it will create a new one.

By now, you may be wondering what the Commandments and sin have to do with love and relationships. For eons, humans have used the Commandments and idea of being sinners as a means to create fear and separation between themselves and the Great Spirit. We have turned against ourselves and others, judging what love is and how to love. We have become the so-called righteous, claiming that our way is the right way and others are wrong, that we should all believe in the same ideas and concepts, and that we should not love ourselves and not take pride in ourselves. As I have mentioned many times already and will continue to mention, this belief is a lie. There is no right or wrong and no judgments from God, but only those based on who you think you are and who you wish to become.

This pre-programming or these beliefs have been pushed for eons by multiple types of propaganda—social, religious, and political—to ultimately create fear and form public opinion. They have affected not just our connection to and relationship with the Universe but our relationships with ourselves and one another.

The powers that be that have attempted to control us. They have tricked us all into believing that God's love is conditional, so our love of one another is also conditional, and that we must only ever give if given—we should only ever give love if love is given to us. They have tricked us into believing that human beings are the only living things capable of giving and receiving love. Through this distorted understanding, we have placed ourselves above all other life forms, but this idea is simply not true. True love (or Divine love, as I like to call it) is unconditional. It does not need or require love in return, and it does not see itself above or below anything. It simply gives without condition. It does not judge or know fear. It loves for the sake of loving and sees all as equal with the Universe because Divine love knows that we are all the same cosmic space filled with dashing protons and neutrons, just each in a different form.

Divine love is why animals, such as cats and dogs, are pets to humans. Those souls chose that experience to show us the love that we hold love within each and every one of us and in each and every living thing in the cosmos. You can shout at a cat or dog, not feed a cat or dog, not show affection to a cat or dog, and they will always forgive you. They will always give you love. They will come to you when you feel down and bring you a toy to play even if you have showered hated on them. These actions are a reflection of the unconditional love we all hold. But we think that because we can think logically or create a piece of art, we are above all over life forms. I ask you to observe your pets, whether they are cats, dogs, or some other animal. Observe enough, and you will see unconditional love.

Before we can start to develop and remember what love truly is, we must redefine our understanding of it. As with most things in the physical realm, to do so, we must break it all down, unlearn what we think we know, and create space for a new understanding.

I must express that what you have been taught to believe and embody as your truth was all taught out of love. Even if there were distortions, your parents, teachers, and even some religious figures could only pass on what they have been taught or perceived from their human experience and the material available to them. You must remember that many of these leaders grew up without the internet. There was no YouTube, and many libraries didn't have the information that is openly available to us now. Everyone did their best from their perspective and experiences. Bless them all, for each has been valuable to your understanding at this moment.

The first stage of redefining love is to redefine the love of the Great Spirit and the Universe. Ultimately, the relationship we have with the Divine and ourselves reflects onto our human experience.

Despite what you have been taught, the Great Spirit does not and will not ever judge or forsaken you. Nothing you can do or say will ever change that. It's only ever been us judging ourselves. This may be hard to take in, but its Divine truth. The Great Spirit does not require anything from you—not love, not money, not material possessions, not anything. It does and will love you regardless.

There is no hell. The Great Spirit does not and will not ever need you to pay anything to be forgiven, to feel and experience its Divine love. Nor can you pay your way into heaven as it's a level of conscious rather than this idea of being a physical place. This idea is yet another distortion of the message used by the powers that be to create money, control, and power. Because of this distortion of the love and relationship the Divine has with us and us with it, we have simply placed ourselves into this thing or place called hell and become our own biggest rivals. But you will always have a place with the Great Divine because you are a part of it.

The Universe is not against us. When we remove the labels and judgments, we begin to see that every person and living thing and its experience was created for us or them to develop further on a soul level. The Universe is simply here to help us co-create our personal experiences with the Great Spirit.

With this old-but-new yet basic understanding of the love and relationships the Universe has with us and us with it, it's time to release all fears and judgments against the Great Spirit, others, yourself, and the Universe. The time has come to remove all separation from the Universe, ourselves, and others. It's time to see past all ego judgments about backgrounds, races, religions, skin colors, languages, sexual orientations, and past actions and instead see and show only the Divine inner light that shines from everything in the universe.

Just like our relationship with the Universe, we have separated ourselves from one another, turning statements of Divine love and harmony into ego and fear. This change has been made and continues to be made through mass public manipulation, mainstream media, and most importantly, organized religion and the entertainment industry. Through this programming, we have distorted what love really is, which has distorted our relationships and love of ourselves. We subconsciously act of fear and ego, causing control, abuse, insecurities, self-judgment, judgment of others, and many of the relationship issues we see in the world today, as well as constantly attracting those vibrations back to us unconsciously with undesirable results.

As your vibration rises through experience and remembrance, you naturally come into alignment with the mind of the Divine Spirit and your higher self, rising into the heart space and beyond and becoming conscious of your creative Divine tools and Divine will. Just like we did with the Commandments and sins, it is time to release and let go of any shame, guilt, revenge, embarrassment, anxiety, or resentment. Holding on to these emotions will only keep you in a vibration of fear. It won't progress your journey, and it serves no purpose in moving forward or in your creative process.

When I say let go and release, I mean let go of *everything*: all the sins, the failure to live up to the Commandments, the so-called bad things you've ever done or said. You are now beginning to see the true purpose of those experiences, which was to simply develop and grow your soul understanding of who you are, the pure Divine light you are, and what you came here to do or be. When you let go, you will create a new vibration that brings with it a new life experience. Then you will go into a space of faith, Divine love, and understanding.

The angels and the Universe are calling you now to stop judging yourself and others. The experiences you have had was one you wanted and needed to develop your understanding of who you are and who you wish to be. Find it in your heart to love and forgive yourself and others who may have hurt you or done you wrong. Forgive yourself for the times you didn't live up to expectations (whether they be yours or others') and each and every person and event. All souls are angels from the heavens, and all have agreed with you to give you that experience or event. It was a mutual agreement. So, forgive, let go, and release. You are not a bad person, and neither are they. We are just finding our way home. Yes, we sometimes get a little lost, but remember this: "Sometimes one must lose themselves to find themselves." You are loving and always loved, protected, and guided. You are never judged by your angels or the Great Source.

Now that you have started to forgive release and let go, it's time to show yourself some love. Tell yourself you are awesome, that you are not and never have been a bad person, that you are a soul having a human experience, that you are loved and loving, that you are perfect, and that you are whole, guided, and protected always! Now breathe for one minute and smile.

Remember to always show yourself love, even in the busy day-to-day life. Treat yourself to something, go for a walk at your favorite location, listen to some uplifting music, gather with friends, laugh with family, meditate, or simply take a day off work. Know you are deserving of it and be grateful that the Universe has your back.

When you truly love who and what you are, you will change your relationships with others. You start to see with Divine eyes and move out of the vibration of fear into love, a.k.a., the heart space, and thus, others start to see that light too.

As you start to understand the love that you are literally made from and the love around you, then you will start to attract more harmonious, Divine, loving relationships with not just family friends but also people and nature. All the insecurities, worries, anxiety, and judgment of yourself and others will begin to fade, allowing you to step into your Divine power, create more space for loving, joyful Divine creativity, and see all life as a part of the whole—all Divinity in expression.

As you start to raise your vibration by moving into the heart space and higher chakras, the people around you will inevitably change. Those who hurt you will disappear, old friends who don't support your current path and vibration will fade, and new souls will appear—souls that resonate with your new energetic vibration. All this change is for spiritual soul growth and because of possible soul contracts with those who you newly attract.

They say you know when you have a soul contract with someone because you get that feeling of knowing each other for years when it's been only ten minutes in Earth time. It feels like you've known them all your life. I've often thought that there was a reason for this feeling of instant familiarity because I am a firm believer in everything happening for a reason.

You may find that as you become more conscious of who you truly are, you change jobs or locations. It's possible you will be a totally new person. Just remember, that which fades from you is not anything bad or negative. It's simply that those people, that job, or that place has taught you all you need to know, and you are moving forward on your path and them on theirs. As the age-old saying goes, "When one door closes, another door opens." But we must also remember that for a new door to open, an old door must close. If we want something but are clinging on to something we fear losing, that thing we want will evade us until we let go and let flow.

As you forgive and start to open yourself to true Divine love, you will begin to stop attracting those negative relationships, and you will notice that your relationship to the All and your connection to mother Earth, the Great Divine, and others improve.

Just like healing ourselves, we can send Mother Earth love to thank her for all that she has endured. As we heal ourselves and the world, it becomes a domino or ripple effect. I discuss this in more detail later, but in simple terms, when we become awakened and start to remember who and what we truly are—that we come from a space of Divine love—we become a stone in the pond, the ripple (our energy) expanding and touching others, which in turn causes them to awakened and remember more and more who they truly are and who they are meant to be.

Not only do our relationships with nature animals and people become stronger, but so does our connection to the spirit world. We all have angels, fairies, dragons, and many more spirit guides and helpers watching over us and guiding us, even if we don't think we do or are not aware of them. I will discuss angels a little later, but for now, just be open to the idea. There are plenty of books on fairies, dragons, and elementals. I encourage you to research these spirit guides because they really do help strengthen the connection with your higher self and the Great Divine. Diana Cooper has written some great books about his spirit helpers, and there are many other resources out there.

As we start to reconnect with ourselves and the Universe, we start to open and strengthen our connection to the angels and the spirit realm. They can help us with forgiveness and understanding, guide us, and keep us safe and protected. As with everything in the Universe, you must give your permission. As the age-old saying goes, "Ask, and you shall receive."

As you release, forgive, and let go, reconnecting to your true essence and your angels and guides will move love and remembrance into your heart space, and your love for yourself and others will grow. Your love for all life will grow, your spiritual gifts will begin to shine forth, and your purpose will start to become clear. The difficult relationships you once found yourself attracting will fade, and you will start to attract relationships with those who share your new, higher vibration, bringing more loving, harmonious experiences, and companionship. I'm not saying you will do it in a day, but have faith, trust yourself and the angels, and know you are healing. You are guided and on the path of your grandest joy.

The Message about Love and Relationships

All are created from and out of love. God is Love, and love is unconditional, which may be hard for people to understand. Relationships are good indicators for you to see and express the love you think you are and the love you wish to be, as well as mirrors reflecting the love you are or areas in which you need to heal. They don't just show us areas we need to heal but also reflect inner aspects we have hidden away or forgotten. Some souls come to us as mirrors of what we are capable of. They come to show us our potential in creativity, power, strength, and faith.

Relationships were created for us to show and express the love that we are and the love we wish to be. Love is not a possession or obsession. This idea is an illusion created by the powers the be, coupled with our own imagination of fear. Only when we learn to love ourselves will we attract the love we desire.

Relationships and our love in relationships not only express the love with hold within us but the love we give to the world.

The commandments were never meant as a command from God as God will never command due to infringement of freewill but simply guidelines on how you can live your best life, and experience all the amazing love filled opportunity life has to offer without creating harm to yourself, and without creating karmic energy of which you will need to come back to earth to heal.

As you slowly become more aware and raise your vibration you will begin to notice that you will naturally morally align with these guidelines as they are naturally higher vibration understandings.

There are no sins which you are going to be judged for, and no hell you are going to be burning in, the sins where given to humanity again as guidelines on how to avoid any experiences on earth which may cause harm mentally and physically to yourself or others, to avoid the creation of negative energy in the body which causes illnesses and diseases but also to avoid creating individual, collective and cosmic karma as humans did in times gone by.

The world has distorted the truth of love and its purpose, this distortion has in turn created a distorted view of love within the collective consciousness. Through the remembrance of your divine nature you can heal this distorted perspective of love and bring forth the true understanding of its creation and purpose in the physical.

Most of us have struggled with love, to feel it and understand it because we have no understood what it truly is. When we redefine the experience and characteristics of love then we can start to define our own earthly experiences. It is through this misunderstanding of love as to why we have so many relationships and lack of self-love issues.
Through divine remembrance you will begin to see the changes in your personal relationships and experience the true expression of love. When this happens no longer will you ever go back to experiences of neglect, abuse, lack of self-love.

Love is simply the highest vibrational frequency we can resonate at, this is the vibrational frequency which your soul is striving to elevate too, because once in this vibration, the soul is closest   to   the   mind   of   God.

Angels, Ascended Masters, Elementals, and Dragons

Angels have been known since time. They were written about in ancient texts, spoke about in ancient dialogues throughout all religions and non-religions, and depicted in images found around the world. Despite what religious leaders and the media have taught us to believe, angels are not myths or associated with religion only. They present with us all. Our very essence is their very essence. We come from the same source as the angels: The Great Spirit. Just like each and every one of us, angels are a separate but unified expression of the Great Source, each with certain specialized abilities.

Regardless of religion or belief system, stories of angels are a part of our heritage, the fabric that makes up human history. They have been and always will be here to assist humanity in whatever we wish to heal, create, or improve.

The reason why people have found it hard to believe in angels is because of the false programming of "seeing is believing." We only believe in something if we see it. If this is true, then what can be said with oxygen? We don't see the air we breathe, and we can't touch it, but it's there. If it weren't, we wouldn't be either. Scientists have equipment that can read the oxygen in the air, so we know it's there. Just because we cannot visually see it doesn't mean it isn't there.

Although there have been accounts of people interacting and seeing angels, angels operate at a much higher level than us. They are far beyond the density of the physical world and will only show themselves in physicality when we repeatedly miss a message or to protect us from immediate danger. They do always show themselves as a light being with wings but could be a person who magically appears helps you or gives you a message and then suddenly disappears.

Angels and guides all work through imagination. The imagination is the soul's playground. Due to the high vibration of angels, it's easy for them to access you through that medium. It's hard at first to get your head around this idea because we have been taught that the imagination is nothing but mental concept which merely servers no bigger purpose to your life experience and spiritual understandings. But as you read this book and uncover the truth of your soul, you will start to understand that the imagination has far more power and purpose than we have been taught to believe.

Science has proved that through imagining, you can cause the body to feel that sensation. Let's say you imagining yourself in a hot place even though you are sitting in a cold room. With a solid imagination and focus, you can cause the body to react as though it were in that hot place, this is because the brain can't tell what is real or imaginary as all is just vibrational frequency, there are plenty of books explaining this concept. Imagination is also how the law of attraction works. This information is not a secret. There have been so many accounts of people using their imaginations to manifest things they wish to see in their lives, this has been well known as using the "law of attraction". Take this book, for instance. I saw it in my mind's eye before it even got published. The point I am making here is that imagination is a tool we can use to access the higher energies and a tool we have been gifted to connect and create!

The imagination is the tool we use to access the angelic realm. Remember that just because you are using your imagination, that doesn't mean the angelic realm isn't there or that your interaction isn't really happening as reality is simply a projection of one's inner consciousness. Regardless of who you are and what you have done, we are all worthy of connecting with God and the angels. We all have angels and guides assigned to us, ready and waiting to help us with our every need. All you need is to believe, trust, and have faith that they are always there for you.

The thing we forget is that we must *ask* for whatever we need, which includes assistance from the angels. The law of free will states no one can bring you harm or do anything to you unless they have your permission, nor can you do anything to them unless you have their permission. However, I must note here that although you can't do anything to anyone without their permission, you can hold positive visions for them. But don't worry. I'll get into this idea a later on.

We must ask for everything in the world. If you want the angels to help you or guide you, then you must ask and be specific. What is it that you are asking for? When do you want it? How do you want it? For instance, just the other day, I was driving along and asked my angels for a sign that I was on my true-life path. I asked for a car to have a license plate containing "777" (one of my favorite combinations) in the next half hour. Within ten minutes, I saw not one but two license plates containing "777." I smiled, acknowledged, and sent gratitude to the angels and the Great Spirit for getting what I had asked for. As Abraham and Esther Hick say, "Ask, and it shall be given."

A little trick I do is I don't ask the angels for much very often, and I say thank you (a lot). You see, gratitude is one of the highest human vibrational emotions. When expressing gratitude, you are coming from your heart space, which is where your true essence lays, where your gifts can be remembered and accessed, and where your creative energy is most potent.

When sending gratitude to the angels, not only is it a vibration of love but a reverberation of faith. You are not asking because you know that "ask, and it shall be given," so naturally, you become open in gratitude and faith, which is the perfect place to be when receiving anything. When I express gratitude, I say, "Thank you, angels and ascended masters, for a sign of your presence," and I smile. In this instance, I don't ask for a time. I just go about my day being open with no expectation of how it will come or when it will come.

A point to remember is just to be open to receiving rather than holding onto expectations of the outcome, thinking about how it's going to come or when. Just know that the angels have heard your request and that it already has been fulfilled. You are just aligning with the vibration of your own request. When we put an expectation on things, it can prevent us from getting what we asked for. Why? It boils down to faith and Divine love. Resistance creates resistance, and flow creates flow.

When we are closed to receiving or have a lack of faith or a lack of belief, it creates an energy of a lower vibration than that of faith and gratitude. When coming from this lower energy, we stop our openness to the messages of the angels and Great Source, as well as prevent ourselves from receiving all the joy and gifts the angels, ascended masters, and Great Source is waiting to gift to us. The world is but a mirror of the soul and subconscious thoughts and beliefs.

How do the angels communicate with us? Angels are always trying to get out attention, even before we have become aware of their presence and support. They do so in many ways. One sign is repeating numbers. Numbers have meaning. Nothing is just random. When you're thinking of something, such as, "I am I going to get paid well, and then see '888' on a license plate, a train ticket, a receipt, etc.," it means complete financial support from the universe. Be open to receiving and listening to the inner intuitive prompts. The message will always depend on the question and context.

Angels and the Universe use not only numbers to get our attention or to send us messages. They use many different forms, such as channeling through friends or a stranger. A good example of this channeling is one of my personal experiences. The following is an experience which to this day I hold as an immensely personal and profound experiences I have had when it comes to the angels and Spirit guides. I don't speak of this experience, but I feel it will help bring a better understanding to how angels and guides come into our lives, and also the angels would like me to share it with you. To save any confusion and for confidentially will use made up names for this explanation.

Not long after my mental breakdown, I was at Jack's a friend's house with Claire a good friend of mine. A group of us was sitting around a table, talking about random things. Then my friend John knocked on the door. We could tell when he walked into the room that he had been drinking. John sat down and joined me Jack Claire and Johns partner Tracey at the table joined us in the conversation, and we got talking about my band. At first, it just seemed like a normal conversation a drunken friend and I would have, but in an instant, the energy completely changed. It felt like we'd been put in a high vibration bubble where there was only him and me (John). Nothing else seemed to exist. John ended up talking about how the band was a distraction to my purpose, and that now was the time to get to work, so to speak. I don't know what it was, but this statement got my utmost attention.

During this time, the energy was so strong that my good friend Claire, who was open to the spiritual world, felt it too. It was so intense that she had to turn away.

As my drunken friend spoke, I immediately got this inner feeling that I wasn't talking to him but to my guides. It was a feeling that even now I can't put into words. I couldn't peel my eyes away. I was fixed upon every word he said, my heart ringing with every word. That was when I knew I was communicating with a higher source. Whilst this conversation was going on, Jack and Tracey we having their own discussion totally unaware of the nature of the conversation I was having, it was like for the moment although I could see I was at the table that I was in fact not there, but instead in this little bubble with my guide where by Claire accidently found herself in, I believe this was because she too was open to spirit, Neither Tracey nor Jack acknowledged the angelic interaction. I had always believed in angels, but this moment was a turning point in the strength of my belief in angelic forces.

The conversation had ended, and it was like we got sucked back into the room, the bubble had been popped and there We all were all sitting at the table, John clueless to the words he had just spoken everyone talking away, and my once-wise drunken friend now back to pointless drunken ramblings. My friend Claire and I looked at each other in amazement. We really didn't know what to say to each other, so we just smiled.

That experience is an example of how angels use the vessel of a friend or stranger to give you a message. I often say that when you drink, you open yourself up to the spirit world. Why else would they call drinks "spirits"?

The Universe delivers its divine guidance through all mediums. Let's use the TV, for example. Let' say you're watching TV and asking the angels or the Great Spirit, "Should I go somewhere?" Then, suddenly, there is a program or ad that says something like, "Yes, getaway," or "Time for your getaway." The Great Source is infinite and, therefore, uses infinite mediums to communicate.

Let's use the example of music. You could be listening to Spotify while thinking about a certain thing or asking a certain question. Then a song comes on confirming or answering your thoughts. Remember, the Universe doesn't need you to speak words. Yes, the spoken word adds energetic momentum, but merely thinking that question or saying it in your head is enough. The Universe doesn't understand words but goes on the feeling—the energy being emanated at that moment.

Mediums that angels or the Great Source might use are the TV, music, books, the whisper of the wind, nature (spirit animals), and social media. (Yes, those in power never anticipated that we would use social media as a medium to spread inner wisdom and reawaken souls to who they really are.) Messages can come through billboards, newspapers, or people, be they strangers, relatives, or friends, not to mention intuition and dreams.

Be open to receiving when you ask because if you don't express specifics in your asking or gratitude, then you have said to the Universe, "You can use any medium and send me a message whenever you want and however you want." If you want answers or guidance straight away, then express that. You can literally ask for anything, be it support, guidance, knowledge, help with healing, universal wisdom, the best path, or advice. Many angels, ascended masters, and higher evolved beings (HEBs) are ready and waiting for us to call upon them.

It's worth noting here that there are no such things as demons or the devil, but there are lower vibrational energies that thrive when we are in a lower state. They can attach to your aura and distort your emotions, as well as cut off your connection to the Great Source, but the truth is that we do this to ourselves without any outside influence. When calling upon the angels, always ask that the guidance be of pure Divine wisdom, honesty, and accuracy, and for the greatest good of all involved. By doing so, you are taking your power back and allowing only the angels of pure higher divine wisdom to guide and support you. Remember to always state, "Only that which is for your and the Universe's highest good." This statement will also cut and energic bonds or attachments you may have from this lifetime and others, allowing you to release, forgive, and move forward, which is what life is all about.

As I mentioned earlier, there are many angels and ascended masters ready to help us uncover our Divine gifts, purpose, and will. But just to keep things simple, we'll look at the main archangels and their specialties. Remember, angels are omnipresent, meaning that they can be in two or three places at once. Just because Joe Blows are asking them for guidance doesn't mean you can't too.

Archangels are considered to very powerful spiritual beings that have captured our attention for centuries. The prefix "arch" means "ruling" or "chief" in Greek. Religious texts refer to archangels as being at a high level in the celestial hierarchy. While the exact number of archangels is unknown, many traditions and faiths reference seven archangels. Who these seven are is also a source of debate varying from faith to faith. Many scriptures tell of the archangels' great abilities as healers and guides, intervening with assistance in many of life's challenging situations.

The main archangels we will discuss are Michael, Uriel, Gabriel, Raphael, Chamuel, Jophiel, Ariel, Azrael, Metatron, and Sandolphon.

Archangel Michael, whose name means "he who is as God," is most often thought of as the angel of protection and the most powerful of all the angels. He is considered a leader within the angelic realm and a patron angel of righteousness, mercy, and justice. He can be called upon for protection, assistance, and guidance, including courage, direction, energy, vitality, all aspects of life purpose, motivation, space clearing, spirit releasement, worthiness, and self-esteem. The best way to invoke Michael is to simply call upon him or imagine yourself cocooned in a protective bubble of blue light. You could also simply say, "Thank you, Archangel Michael, for protecting me from [name]."

Archangel Uriel is known as the angel of wisdom. He shines the light of God's truth into the darkness of confusion. Uriel means "God is my light" or "fire of God." Call upon Uriel for help-seeking God's will before making decisions, learning new information, solving problems, and resolving conflicts. He is also good for boosting libido. People also turn to him for help letting go of destructive emotions such as anxiety and anger.

Archangel Gabriel's name means "God is my strength." One of the two archangels specifically named in the Bible—in both the Old and New Testament—she is often portrayed as holding a trumpet and the only female archangel, although I do want to mention here that angels have no gender, they will appear to each in a manner which the person can relate. Archangel Gabriel is the messenger angel, acting as a messenger of God. She helps writers, teachers, journalists, and artists convey their messages, find motivation and confidence, and can even help to promote and market their skills. She also assists people with overcoming issues of fear and procrastination in communication, as well as in all areas related to children.

Archangel Raphael, whose name means "God heals," is the archangel designated for physical and emotional healing. Archangel Raphael helps clear away fears that may be negatively affecting your health. He can help reduce addictions and cravings and is powerful in healing other injuries and illnesses, with cures often taking effect immediately. The best way to invoke Raphael is to imagine an emerald light surrounding your being and breathe that light in. If you have a certain health concern, then imagine the area covered in Raphael's light, and ask Raphael to help to heal. Be open and allow.

Archangel Chamuel's name means "he who sees God." His mission is to bring peace and the energy of love to the world, and as such, he protects the world from fear and lower-vibrating, negative energies. He is believed to be all-knowing, seeing the interconnectedness between all things. Archangel Chamuel assists us in finding the strength and courage to face adversity when it seems we have none left. He can also help find items that are lost, find solutions to problems, and find important parts of our lives, such as life purpose, romantic relationships, new jobs, and supportive friendships. Lastly, Archangel Chamuel also helps us to uncover the divine love we hold within ourselves and how to express that in the external world.

Archangel Jophiel's name means "beauty of God." She helps us see and maintain beauty in life and supports us in thinking beautiful thoughts and staying positive, as well as in creating and manifesting beauty in our surroundings and hearts. Archangel Jophiel watches over artists, supporting the creation of beautiful art and helping us slow down and bring calm to our lives. She heals negativity and chaos and helps tame the ego and bring organization to a place or situation. When seeking wisdom or a shift in perspective, Archangel Jophiel is the one to call to uplift you and help you see things from a different point of view.

Archangel Ariel's name means "lion or lioness of God." Her role is to protect the Earth and its natural resources, and all wildlife, and she is always available with support and guidance for any activities that involve environmentalism and protecting, healing, rejuvenating, or maintaining our environment. Archangel Ariel assists with healing injured animals, working closely with Archangel Raphael. It is believed that she also works to oversee the order of the physical universe, including all planets, the sun, the moon, and the stars. She provides insight and opportunities to expand our awareness and experience. Given that Archangel Ariel is watching over the Earth's natural resources, she can also be especially helpful in ensuring our needs for food, water, shelter, and other supplies are met, as well as bring abundance in all forms, be it spiritual or material.

Archangel Metatron is a powerful angel who teaches people how to use their spiritual power for good while recording their choices in the Universe's great archive (known either as God's book of life or the Akashic record). Some believe that Metatron is one of only two angels (the other being Archangel Sandolphon) who were first humans before joining the Divine providence. It is believed he was the prophet Enoch from the Torah and the Bible before ascending to heaven and becoming an angel. Metatron's experience living on Earth as a person gives him a special ability to relate to people who want to connect with him.

Archangel Sandolphon is the archangel of music, poetry, and prayer. Sandolphon receives and delivers prayers to the Divine so that they are clearly heard and answered. Call upon Sandolphon if you are having doubts that your prayers are being heard, and he will help update you on the progress of your request and tune into anything you need to do to transform your prayers into positive blessings unfolding in your life.

There are many more angels and ascended masters who you can call upon for help, guidance, and support in whatever way you need, including the following:

- Raziel
- Lord Ganesh
- Buddha
- Master Jesus
- Odin
- Quan Yin
- Mother Mary
- Cernuous
- Lord Kuthumi
- Great White Chief

Although I have examples of angels and some of their aura colors, they will ultimately come to you in a form, image, and color that resonates most deeply with you. Angels know us well, and they know how to get our attention. They will choose a form, color, or shape that you can relate to. For instance, let's say you call upon Archangel Michael. You may see him in a different outfit or with an aura color other than blue. Know that however he appears is perfectly fine. Just go with what you feel or is being shown to you. Angels are omnipresent, meaning that they can be in more than one place at once, so don't worry if your friend says she sees Archangel Michael or other angels in different color light lights or if she has been working with AA Michael too.

There are many resources with more information about elementals, dragons, unicorns, angels, ascended masters, and HEBs. I call upon and use all of them in all situations. I've also found that angel, oracle, and tarot cards are a great way to connect and strengthen your connection with the angels. They're also a great way to get to know the angels and their energies. The more you call upon and use the angels, the more you will notice their signs and energies.

Not only are there angels and ascended masters, but there are also elementals, dragons, and unicorns, each with their own energy signature and various gifts and abilities to offer us. Again, there are a lot of resources and information out there. If you wish to know more, ask your guides or angels to guide in the right direction so you can understand their different energies and what they have to offer us.

Angels have been around since time began, they have helped many civilizations both here on earth, on other planter systems in the universe and in other dimensions. They are not just a myth created here on earth. Archangels not only help to bridge the connection between humans and the but also are specialized extensions of God, each archangel has an aspect of which it specializes, to re-cap the above, AA Michael specializes in protection, love and order. AA Raphael specializes in healing, AA Uriel specializes in confidence of life purpose, helps you to shine your light in the darkest of places. Whether you connect with angels for guidance, or for their specialized talent remember they have been created by God to help heal guide and mentor you in your human experience and soul discovery, along with your spirit guides and heavenly soul family so use them.

The message from the angels is that "you are not alone, you are not here randomly, and you have a purpose and the whole of the heavens waiting to assist you in your soul lessons and journey". All you need do is call upon them and ask for what you need. Heavenly support is always there and ready to get started with improving your life experience.

The Message about Angels, Ascended Masters, Elementals and Dragons

Angels have been mentioned all over the world in many different religions. You don't have to be religious to connect with the angels. They are and always will be around you.

The law of free will prevents angels from intervening unless you give them permission. Once you ask, the angels will get to work on your behalf.

Angels get out attention in many ways, and they take many forms, not just light beings with wings. Anyone can connect with the angels and receive the messages. You just need to be open and willing. Again, believing is seeing.

There are different types of angels all play unique roles, the main ones we are conscious of are our spirit guides and the archangels.

Although we call them ascended masters they too are angels, the only reason we call them ascended masters is simply because those souls unlike archangels have lived physically lives upon mother earth, so they are aware of the trials and tribulations the human experience can bring.

Angels are omnipresent, meaning they can be a multiple place's at once, and they can change their appearance, although the aura very rarely changes.

One angelic experience may differ to another, angels know us well, in fact they have worked with us for eons, and some of us have come down from the angelic realm.

Angels very rarely will show up in the physical as physical life like beings, not to say it doesn't happen because it does but more often than not they will show themselves through a sign or an deep inner knowing, or maybe through a drunk friend or relative like my experience, needless to say like Great Spirit they work in many ways, so don't place any expectation on how you think the experience should or will be just allow it to simply BE.

Angels and Spirit Signs

Angels and the Great Source uses all kinds of mediums to communicate with us because we all have different learning methods—or I should say, remembering methods. The angels know that we are all different and tend to send messages in a way that you will notice more easily, often through the inner voice and imagination. Then again, if the message is not clear enough, you can literally ask for a sign and the way you would like that sign to show itself.

This chapter will look at just a small list of the way's angels communicate with us.

Dreams

You may have dreams of visiting an angel or an angel visiting you. Angels often use our sleep state to communicate the message they want for us to here. Dreams are ideal because we don't have the voice of the ego doubting ourselves or the hustle and bustle of everyday life. Whenever you dream of angels or ascended masters, be open to the message they are giving you. Just make sure you set the intention that you will remember anything important that you will need to know.

Keep a dream journal to record your dreams. At the time, a dream might seem like it has no relevance to you or your current energy, but that is the ego trying to trick you. Dreams reflect important messages from the subconscious and the angelic realm. When we focus and set an intention to understand our dreams, the meanings become more meaningful.

Just the other week, my friend and I went to a beautiful cottage for a weekend retreat—one we both needed. It was heavenly. It was so quiet, and we could see green grass for miles. One night, while my friend was cooking us a vegan pizza, I fell asleep—I mean, it was, like, three or four in the morning— and I dreamed about a visit from an archangel. Even now, I still remember talking to an archangel (I believe it was Ariel). She was stunningly beautiful. Her eyes like shone electric blue like the cosmos, her hair looked like the sands of an untouched beach, and she wore delicate and beautiful robes. She was engulfed by a pure Divine light that seemed to emanate all around her, I remember talking intensely to her. I can't remember what we talked about, but I'll never forget the vibe she had. It was like we were long-time friends. I recall laughing and joking in among the serious talk. Then, while I was in full flow, my friend shook me and woke me up. There she was, standing and smiling stunningly with pizza in her hand. I said to her, "Oh, wow! You just woke me up when I was in the middle of a conversation with the angels." She laughed and said that I was saying something in my sleep, but she couldn't remember what it was, and neither could I. It was a message for the soul, and I know it will come into more light when the divine moment is perfect.

This moment is just one example of the way's angels communicate with us, and I have had many similar experiences. Don't take your dreams as randomness. Nothing is random.

Feathers

Feathers a personal favorite for me because I always feel like the angels are standing all around me, rejoicing and celebrating.

Angels often get our attention using things like feathers or coins. These objects are Divine signs from the angels to say, "Hey, you're on the Divine path home. Stay here, and you will create your heaven on Earth." They are a sign to say you are right where you need to be and doing what you need to do. Anytime I come across one of these signs on my path, I first ask myself, "What I was thinking before seeing this sign?" because these signs can come as an answer to a certain question you asked. Or, they could simply be an answer to your prayers asking your angels for a sign. As great souls like Abraham Hicks say, "Ask, and you shall receive."

Feathers can be of any color. They don't have to be pure white. Ultimately, they remind you that angels are by your side, loving and supporting you. When you find a feather or coin in a particularly unusual place, it is a powerful sign. Heed it, accept it, and be grateful for it.

Music and Lyrics

Angels also work through music. I often find when I am asking a question or speaking of a subject with positive energy, and the next song that comes on my phone, CD, or radio has relevance to what I have been thinking or talking about. Angels love music and often use it to talk to us, so listen closely. That next track might just be giving you the guidance you have been asking for.

The Great Spirit and angels use all mediums to communicate with us, and music is often a common one because we all like music, and we all relate to it. What better way to deliver a message? I've often had times when I was driving along and decided to ask a question to my angels or the Great Spirit. Normally, its "If there are any messages the angels with to give me, then I am open receiving them." I thank the angels and allow the Universe to do its work. Then a certain track comes on my iPhone that either answers the question directly or has a heavy relation to my thoughts or feelings at that moment.

Cloud Formations

You may be driving along, sitting on a train, or walking somewhere only to look up and see what seems like a silhouette of an angel in the sky. What a beautiful sign! These cloud formations are messages from your angels saying, "We are here. You are not alone. We love you and will support you always." They could also be a confirmation of something you have asked for. Just remember to be open to receiving and don't dismiss these Divine synchronicities as just random or coincidence. Nothing in this world is random or coincidence.

The clouds don't have to be in the of an angel but can take many forms, such as spirit animals, shapes, or symbols. Just know that they are a message for you.

Scents or Perfumes

Angels use sweet smells to get our attention, such as the smell of flowers or chocolate. Although scents are used by the angels and the Great Source, it's often either a sign from a passed loved one or scents of the Divine feminine. Angels, especially those of a feminine energy, tend to have a scent linked to them. For instance, Mother Mary is closely linked to the smell of roses. It could also be that you were missing someone, so that person gave you a sign that they were there with you. Maybe someone has passed recently, and you may smell their favorite perfume or scent. Either way, take these beautiful scents as signs that your loved ones or the angels are close.

TV and Media

We have all had those moments where we're chilling with friends or sitting with family, and then an ad comes on the TV with a direct answer to something you asked in your head or heart. That is a message from your Angels.

A Stranger on the Internet, or a Random Encounter

Nothing is ever random. Angels can and do deliver messages and signs through others, be it a friend or a stranger on social media or a random encounter when you're out and about. That is one of the reasons it is said that we should "bless all that comes to us, for each is an angel sent from the heavens to you." They are there to either give you a message or experience or to protect you.

Always be completely open when asking the universe for a sign. If you want something specific, then ask for that.

For more advice and information on angels and ascended masters, I recommend looking into the work of Kyle Gray, Diane Cooper, Sonia Choquette, Radleigh Valentine, and Melanie Beckler. They are amongst my favorites.

The Message about Angels and Spirit Signs

We all have angels, so use them and be open to their guidance and signs. Above all, trust that you are not alone. Your guides and the angels are always close by, waiting for you to call upon them and thank them. You can share angels with your friends, family, and many others, but if you can't, that is completely okay.

The angels and guides will get your attention in ways that are personal to you. It could be an item, a person, a scent, or showing themselves as an object or remembered scene.

Food, Health and Exercise

"Healthy thoughts create a healthy body. Unhealthy thoughts create an unhealthy body." As we go deeper and remember more and more of who we truly are, our lifestyles, diets, and habits change naturally as we raise our vibration, just like with family, friends, love, and relationships.

Many of the health issues we face are created as a result of our unhealthy and negative thought patterns and societal conditioning. Our health conditions are a direct result of what we ingest and put inside our bodies. It's causes and effect. Unhealthy foods, alcohol, and other recreational drugs are major factors in the diseases we experience.

There is currently so much disharmony within humanity's spiritual, mental, emotional, and physical health. It doesn't help that mainstream media promote unhealthy foods, supplements, and synthetic harmful chemicals and substances everywhere we turn, with healthier options often being much more expensive and less readily accessible. Toxins such as alcohol and tobacco are promoted excessively. Heavy metals, pesticides, and other poisons are continuously sprayed into our atmosphere, onto our foods, and into our water supply. Not to mention that government services and their employees are heavily discouraged from speaking the truth and are often threatened with losing their jobs if they speak out. Proper healing and health advice are frowned upon and even illegal within the allopathic community. But let's not forget that even public services are businesses, and they must make money.

Responsibility of The Health of Self

Finally, there is the disregard of the responsibility to the self. Yes, we have all done it, and I'm no different, but it's time we take responsibility for ourselves, our health, and our vitality and take care of and showing respect towards other sentient beings and all life on this planet. It is time we take responsibility for our wrongdoings, give back, and work through our karma.

There is a lot of distortion around and within healings methods, a major one being the fact we can heal ourselves and others. The main reason for this distortion is simply control and profit. When you become aware of the fact that the powers that be do not heal people, have never healed anyone, and live in a world of treatment-based thinking, it begs the question, what are their underlying agendas?

Start to home in on your own Divine healing. Remember that Master Jesus once said, "All that I can do, you can do too." He simply meant, "I am you, and you are me." As with all ascended masters who have and are helping show humanity who we truly are, we often miss the messages given, judge, and question the agenda of the person. You have the very same power and abilities to heal as he did. The only difference is the level of faith and trust in your true self-essence and abilities and your understanding of our Divine gifts and the laws of the Universe.

It worth noting that it said that Jesus did not heal all who came to him. That idea is a distortion of the message because not all are allowed to be. Some soul plans may have led souls to choose to have a certain disease to gain a larger perspective of who they are. If Jesus were to heal all who came, those souls would not have felt and gained from the disease as the soul intended. Therefore, it is often said with healers that healing is sometimes not to be given. It could be because a person needs to heal themselves, and another healing that person takes away the experience of self-healing.

The thing with healing is that most of it comes through awareness. There is no need to be hard on yourself and push yourself into something you do not desire to do or are not ready for, such as healthier eating habits, exercising, and spiritual practices. If and when the timing is right for you, these changes will happen naturally.

Awareness of health of the self

When you begin to become aware of yourself and raise your vibrational state, healing will flow naturally, accordingly, and without conscious resistance, including the choice of what foods we eat and what we allow into our bodies. Through awareness of who we truly are, our health and the healing abilities will surface, and you will see that we not only have the ability to heal ourselves and one another but all life and Earth herself.

The main reason and underlying factor of our personal health issues is the disconnection of the higher self—the lack of connection with and awareness of our essence, self, and of love. Only when we understand what love is and what we are can we begin to truly see with Divine eyes by being the Divine itself.

The ego will always be a cloud in your perfect blue sky. Because of our absence of self-love (both consciously and unconsciously), we have neglected and mistreated our bodies, mistreated others, mistreated animals, and mistreated the Earth herself. This disconnect between the essence of the love we are and the forgetting of our connection to spirit is also the main reason for mental health issues in most cases. Mental health issues are also signs of disease within us, further showing that we are disconnected from the higher self.

When great separation is created, we don't feel connected to the whole, others, the Universe, or ourselves. With the illusion of separation comes the feelings of disconnect. Feelings of fear, isolation, and not being worthy.

Reclaiming your divine health

The first stage of moving from a disharmonic vibration to a harmonic vibration regarding health and well-being is simply to remember the love that you are, the love that made you, and the love that made everything you experience in your reality. We are all on this Earth. We are all in this together. We are all united in consciousness. It is this absence of our faith and Divine truth that is the reason for the slaughtering of animals, the destruction of the environment, and the destruction of ourselves. To become healthy, we must start with the heart. We must learn to control our minds in a positive and healthy way and, in doing so, take care of our souls.

If you are not ready in your heart and this idea does not resonate with you, then you aren't ready, which is perfectly fine. You are not being judged. We are all on our own individual journeys of creation, and we are all at our own levels of soul understanding. We will all get there in our own time. But once we open our hearts to health and healing, we become more aware of what our bodies need and what they don't want.

We forget that our bodies talk to us. Why do we experience aches and pains? What are our bodies trying to tell us? What are they communicating? If you truly listen, you will hear exactly what it is saying and how to heal it, you need to *listen*.

Allow yourself some time. Ask your heart—remember, the heart never lies. It speaks to us through senses and how we feel, be it through aches or pains, thoughts, emotions, or even positive feelings such as goosebumps or the release of adrenaline when you experience something truly amazing! It could be that knotted feeling that you get when you face a fear or phobia or when you meet a new love. Our bodies are always communicating.

It's not just the way we treat ourselves that creates disease within us but also what we allow ourselves to believe is possible and how we perceive ourselves in terms of health.

Changing your thoughts and how you perceive yourself, your well-being, your fitness, and your physical appearance directly affects what you choose to create and your overall health. As I said earlier and will continue to repeat (as repetition is key!), our thoughts create our reality. We are always in a state of becoming. Thoughts create our perception, and our perception creates our perspective and vice versa. We must unlearn that which we think we know to rebuild ourselves and our belief systems from the ground up. It is no different when it comes to physical health and vitality.

You are what you think and eat

You may be questioning the cause of health issues that are not the result of your low vibrational thoughts of worry, stress, fear, anxiety, etc. The answers are usually right in front of our faces. The foods we eat, the creams we apply topically to our skin, and the air we breathe all accumulate and contribute. We also must consider that the health issues we experience may ultimately be because we pre-decided to have this experience due to past life karma—not as punishment but to ultimately learn and grow from that particular lesson. It can be hard to comprehend, but those souls who experience certain illnesses or issues will know what they gain—maybe not at first, but the picture always becomes clear. Witnesses to such experiences also gain growth from such lessons.

We can and do bring illness and diseases upon ourselves by repeatedly ignoring our bodies' signals and their intuitive prompts. Below is a story that inspired me from a book called ***Developing Intuition* by Shakti Gawain**. This claimed true story shows the power of ignoring your intuition and how illnesses and diseases can be created for a greater reason.

Not long ago one of my business associates experienced her body getting her attention in a very dramatic way. She has always been a very busy person —

able to accomplish enormous amounts of work in her typical twelve- to fourteen-hour day. She had a lot of energy, loved her work, and was very good at what she did. Many years of working at this face-paced level, however, she began to wear on her body, mind, and soul.

She kept getting intuitive messages that she needed to take off to rest and replenish her body. However, her inner "pusher" kept driving her to accomplish more. She began to get ill, nothing too serious, but it seemed that any cold that was going around would find its way to her. She'd never quite recovered from one cold or flu before she came down with another. Instead of listening to her body and resting, she worked more hours a day to make up for the slow pace due to the illnesses.

Eventually, her body became exhausted, her responses slowed. She was in an automobile accident and had a concussion. Again, she felt that if she worked more hours she could keep up with her work, and so she attempted to do so. Of course, this didn't work either. Eventually, she was in another accident and this time suffered slight brain damage. She *had* to stop. Her body was telling her to slow down, that she needed a break, and she needed to rest. Eventually she took time off work and got the rest she needed and has learned how to create balance in her life.[3]

Because the woman failed to listen to her body and soul when they were communicating to her, they made her listen. This story shows you that your body will attempt to communicate with you over and over to get what it needs. It is up to us to listen.

Another factor to take into consideration when it comes to physical disease manifestations is past life karma. We've

[3]. Shakti Gawain, *Developing Intuition: Practical Guidance for Daily Life*, (Novato, California: Nataraj Publishing, 2002), 122–23.

already discussed past lives and the journey of the soul—how we have many lives as many different characters in many different and unique environments. But let's recap now. Each time we incarnate or reincarnate, we forget who we truly are and what we are doing here, so we can unknowingly create karmic energy.

Let's say that in one lifetime, you were a rich person who often looked down on those with less and treated others disrespectfully. You may find that in your next life, you experience that which you judged others for—you will be the not-so-wealthy person, and someone will treat you badly because of it. This is not a punishment, but a situation created for the soul to gain a complete understanding of that certain energy and enable it to see from a higher perspective. You see, everything we create, and experience is a reflection of what we are. It is what we must understand and develop within us and what we need to heal.

Here's another example. Let's say that in a past life, you disrespected someone for being disabled. Because of this lack of soul understanding of who it is, the soul unknowingly creates karmic energy that needs to be healed, and the only way to do that is through experiencing that disability or a similar situation to gain understanding. Again, this is not a punishment. Nothing in life is judging us or punishing us—well, nothing but ourselves, which are ever-changing. It is simply that the soul created karmic energy that needs to be cleared for it to ascend to higher realms.

As you may be starting to understand, the key to life is sending love and forgiveness to yourself and all those involved. Nothing is against us. Everything is for our highest good so that we can grow and deepen our soul understanding to create in our next moment—that which we think we are and that which we wish to be—in all aspects of our lives.

Unfortunately, humanity has been conditioned to believe that buying the pills, taking the prescriptions, and listening to everyone and everything but the soul (intuition) and the body is healthy when, in fact, most of these drugs only serve to mask that which your soul or body is communicating to you. That masking, in turn, creates more health issues because the body sees is as you not listening, so that bad knee that only twitched is now so severely painful that you struggle to walk. Each time the body or soul communicates to you, it will do so more and more strongly. Everything is there to get us to see from the larger soul perspective.

Alcohol and Drugs

The same can be said with alcohol and legal and illegal drugs (that includes prescription drugs taken illegally). They are pushed on to us to keep us at a vibration where we can be controlled and manipulated.

A lot of people get defensive when you mention alcohol. The world has been taught that alcohol is perfectly fine and is the only way you can "let yourself go" and have fun. This idea is a distortion and a lie. Alcohol was not meant for the body, despite the argument that Jesus gave wine to his disciples. Jesus, like every one of us, was not perfect. But again, people have focused on the person and not the message. Bear in mind that what is written in the religious texts has been rewritten multiple times by humankind, and things have been removed.

Alcohol is simply poison and the leading cause of the mental and physical illnesses and issues many find themselves experiencing. It suppresses human emotion but only for a short time, and then it comes back stronger. It opens your aura to the energies that want to leach off you, lowering your vibration.

Because this information is unknown to the world, people do not protect themselves before going out and drinking, leaving them open to lower energies. That is perhaps why that person you know to be pure love and understanding suddenly becomes unloving and aggressive when they drink. Alcohol feeds the ego. Mainstream media and society will never tell you that because they make a lot of money off alcohol.

Alcohol also promotes separation and fear and enables outside control of the physical and mental self. When under the influence of alcohol, you lower your vibration, puncture holes in your aura (much like the American government is doing with HAARP and the ozone layer) and open yourself up to more consciousness manipulation and control.

The global elites promote using alcohol by constantly advertising it and showing a lot of consumption, saying it is beneficial to your health. This subliminal programming is included in all forms of media, be it TV, magazines, books, or films. All it takes is awareness of the intention to see this manipulation. The powers that be don't want you healthy, happy, or free, and they don't want you to have creative control over your creative Divine gifts. Remember this fact, and you will see the truth of their agenda and, more importantly, the truth of who you truly are. The same truths can be said about not all but most legal and illegal drugs.

If you wish to stop drinking alcohol but struggle due to its addictive qualities, then you can ask the angels to help and support you. Archangels Michael, Raphael, and El Morya can help with cutting any cords of addictions. They can release any lower vibration entities in your vicinity, as well as help with any cravings.

Not all but the majority of the modern mainstream healing methods only serve to mask the issue, not cure the root cause. They simply aim to make money and keep the shackles of control around our beings. If all illnesses and diseases were healed, the powers that be wouldn't make any money and wouldn't have our creative energy to set their creations upon us against our Divine will. But if we focus on the root cause of the issue, then we can bring healing almost instantly.

Let's not forget that the health system is more about making money than the health and care of the people. That part reason why alternative energy healing is mocked—big pharma knows that if we knew the power of these alternative healing methods (such as reiki, crystal healing, sound vibration, plant medicines, and alternatives remedies) and the truth of the power of eating healthy foods such as vegetables and fruits, we wouldn't buy all those corporate, branded pills and foods.

If you wish to know more about other healing modalities, then I employ you to do your own research as there is much information and knowledge out there.

Moving back to wholeness in mind body and Soul

As our awareness grows, we begin to see and understand the many factors that have contributed to our health problems and the health of the world. From this perspective, we can start to change our thoughts about what is healthy for us in both food and medicine and our thoughts about our bodies and health, healing ourselves once and for all.

When your thoughts begin to change around health, well-being, and food, you will inevitably raise your vibration. There are just so many acidic, low-vibration drinks and foods that do no good for our vitality.

I should point out that it is not a race. Everyone is going at their own pace, and that is fine. Some will transition quicker than others, and that's fine. It doesn't make you any more or less of a being. You will change and flow in your own time. Be kind to yourself and be patient. It can be a shock to you and your body to start living in a truly healthy way, but trust and know that you are right where you need to be (reading this book!), and you will transition to higher vibrational thoughts around food, diet, and exercise. Just flow and have faith.

As you do start to transition, you may notice a change in your being. You may start to become more confident and not in an ego way but in a true-love-of-who-you-are way. Old body issues will disappear, mental health will improve, vitality will improve, and overall thirst for life will increases. When you focus your thoughts on a more positive perspective, your body reflects that positivity. You will notice that change, and I guarantee that others will notice it, too, and become curious.

Now that we have a clearer understanding of how we have been creating our health issues, we can start to heal these issues in the same way they were created: through reprogramming the subconscious and turning those once-negative health thoughts into positive thoughts. As Buddha said, "What we think, we become."

The first step is to unlearn what you think you know about healthy foods and diets, creating space for you to take on a new understanding and perspective. Rather than saying things like, "I am depressed," and "I am in so much pain," change these thoughts to "One is witnessing a moment of grey clouds." By referring to yourself as "one," you have immediately taken away the identification to yourself. I believe that is why the richer families, including the royal family, refer to themselves as "one." They know the secret of consciousness and thought and how the statement "I am" is a statement of creation to the Universe. I'll discuss this idea a little later, but for the purposes of this chapter, I will touch upon it quickly.

When you say, "I am," you are making a statement to the Universe. Coupled with strong emotions and action, it creates the perfect three parts of creation, or what I call the holy trinity of creation: thought, word, and action. As I have said repeatedly, we are the creators of our realities. We create every minute of every day. The difference between being awake and asleep in a spiritual sense is being aware of this notion. Most people create unconsciously, and that's what we have all been doing for eons, which is the main reason why we have created so many scenarios and situations that have caused karmic energy. Identifying with what you think you are when you are not that thing will cause you to create that which you think you are. You will create more feelings, thoughts, and events connected to that thing you are identifying with. For example when you repeatedly say you are depressed you are putting out vibrational frequency to the creative universe that you wish to feel and experience the energy of depression, you simply create the experience of that thing you think you are and so by universal law, the universe co-creates with you more thoughts feelings and situations where by you see things which make you depressed, or you have an experience where it makes you depressed, it falls in line with the saying that master Buddha once said "what you think you become" By simply saying, "I am," and then attaching yourself to a lower vibrational statement of that which you think you are, you will only create more health issues and cause them to worsen or persist.

The soul wants you to remember who you truly are, the Divine gifts we all have to heal ourselves, and for you to bring that to your consciousness and heal yourself. Until we see health, foods, and diets in Divine light, the issues and problems will persist.

Just like creating negative health issues, the same process can be used to create a healthy body and a balanced diet. Simply take yourself away from the label you have given yourself. Like I did with the cloud metaphor, the same can be done here. When it comes to our health in mind, body, and spirit, focus only on the statements that are of a positive, higher vibration.

Now all this is not to say you can't feel pain or depression. It simply means that you are identifying with it. By saying, "One is feeling a cloud of depression right now," rather than, "I am depressed," you remove the attachment, which in turn takes away the creative power of that statement, leaving you to put that energy into positive matters.

This vicious circle of unconsciousness creation is the main reason why people make their issues or problems worse. But again, those in power know this. They know about our ability to heal, and they know about the truth of pharmaceutical drugs now how they don't really help us but rather mask our health issues, which in turn creates more health issues and ultimately profit. I am not saying that all doctors, nurses, and so forth don't want to heal you, because most do. They are doing the best they can with the experience and understanding they have. It's more so the global elites that have attempted to keep humanity enslaved by its own Divine consciousness. They care not for the well-being of people or the world. They care only for power, profits, and control.

When we become aware of this situation, we can start to see the healthcare system for what it is and start to heal ourselves without the need for pills and drugs. We can start to heal not only ourselves but also Mother Earth herself through our Divine gifts.

I'm not saying to not follow your doctor's advice or take your medication. I'm simply saying that we need to take some responsibility for our health, the causes of diseases, and ourselves in general. This way, we can stop the vicious cycle of creation and bring our bodies and their health in true alignment with what you truly are. As I've repeatedly said and will continue to say, thoughts attract like vibes. In other words, unhealthy thoughts attract unhealthy thoughts and feelings, and healthy thoughts attract health thoughts and feelings. As Buddha said, "We are what we think we are," and "What we think, we become."

A lot of the beliefs we have are held in the energy centers in the body, which are called chakras. In traditional holistic health, there are seven chakras:

- Crown – Color Violet
- Third eye – Color Indigo
- Throat – Color Blue
- Heart – Color Green

- Solar plexus – Color Yellow
- Navel – Color Orange
- Root – Color red

Figure 3. The seven chakras.

Each chakra is responsible for certain aspects and expressions of the soul. If any one of these energy centers is blocked, it can cause disharmony within the body—this is what is happening collectively within humanity. There have been such repressions in many areas of the psyche that most of these energy centers are not functioning as they should, and they can then create many the health issues we find ourselves facing, as well as many unhealthy beliefs.

We will go through a basic understanding of these chakras to give you an idea of their functions and determine if or where you may have blockages, which will help to heal certain aspects of yourself and negative beliefs and bring forth a new understanding and healing.

The way to see chakras is like little discs like what you would put into a stereo. A CD may seem like it has nothing on it, but when you insert into a CD player, you find out that it holds many tracks. It is the same for our energy centers—they hold certain programming. Each chakra holds different programming. They are where we program certain characteristics and beliefs. If you have a blockage in a certain chakra, it can cause you to lack trust or self-confidence. It depends on which chakra has the blockage. When these chakras function properly, they bring a more unified understanding of who we truly are and our purpose here.

Let's start with the root chakra, which known in Eastern philosophy as the **Muladhara**. The root is where we hold our beliefs about family and self-security (food, water, and shelter). It is the place where we determine our safety in the world. If you constantly feel insecure, unsafe, and unprotected or lack family love and survival needs, then chances are that you have blockages in the root and requires some healing (or reprogramming of that disk). It is the same with overactive chakras. When you come from that energy center alone, it produces aggression and sexual insecurities.

When this chakra is functioning correctly—it is programmed with love rather than fear—it produces a feeling of being grounded, a feeling of safety, and a feeling of protection. Similarly, blockages can show symptoms of a feeling of abandonment, a lack of focus, co-dependency, and restlessness.

In a physical sense, the root chakra is responsible for the organs, bones, and muscles nearest to its location: the spine, anus, skeletal system, pancreas, and feet. If you are suffering in any of these areas, then it is highly likely that you have blockages in the root chakra. When this chakra is function properly, it causes a feeling of and belief in security in regard to survival needs, stability, and grounded-ness, as well as a balance in expressions and emotions of passion and anger.

The **Svadhisthana**, also known as the sacral chakra, is located just above the root and holds programming around emotions, sensations, beliefs, expressions of sexuality and sexual desire, and creativity. If this chakra is imbalanced or blocked, it can cause feelings of depression, low self-esteem, insecurity, unsatisfying relationships (because it is closely linked to the root) detachment, and jealousy, and it is the main source of addiction. An overactive sacral chakra can result in a feeling of overindulgence in sexual desire and being overruled by emotions, which is often perceived as arrogance.

In a physical sense, this chakra energy influences body parts such as the back, kidneys, lymphatic system, bladder, and genitals. If you are suffering from problems in these areas, it is highly likely that you have blockages in the sacral chakra, and healing is to be done. When this chakra is functionally healthily, you feel aligned with source energy for movement, creativity, procreation, sexual desire and pleasure, and balance in relationships.

The **Manipura**, also known as the solar plexus chakra, is located at the top of your abdomen, around the diaphragm area. This chakra is responsible for the programming around self-confidence, feelings of inner bliss, self-assurance, knowledge, wisdom, and decision-making. If this chakra is imbalanced or blocked, it can cause feelings of low self-esteem, a lack of self-control, anxiety, addiction, and the inability to maintain boundaries. If it is overactive, it can produce stubbornness and heavily negative self-judgments.

This chakra is linked to the digestive system, stomach, and intestines. If you have issues with diabetes, stomach ulcers, arthritis, or asthma, there is a high possibility that there is healing to be done in this area. When this chakra is functioning properly, you will have feelings and traits of being able to set boundaries and be assertive. You will have balanced self-confidence, allowing you to know yourself and your flaws but not judge yourself or others critically.

The **Anahata**, also known as the heart chakra, is responsible for programming around love: love for yourself and others, empathy, and harmony. It allows you to feel compassion, give freely, and forgive. The heart chakra interferes with your happiness and relationships. If this chakra is imbalanced blocked, it will show up as a lack of love, compassion, and empathy, the inability to forgive, and feelings of loneliness, shyness, resentment, and suspicion in relationships, both friendships and romantic. An overactive heart chakra can produce neglect of emotional self-care (tolerance of constantly negative behaviors from others), acceptance without discernment, loss of a sense of identity, and being ruled by emotions.

Physically, this chakra is linked with the heart, lungs, and brain. If you are suffering in any of these areas, you may have an imbalanced heart chakra and require. Healing. A balanced heart chakra produces feelings of happiness, joy, understanding, and generosity, as well as understanding and compassion towards oneself and others. It also attracts balanced romantic relationships and enables empathy and forgiveness.

The **Vishuddha**, also known as the throat chakra, is responsible for the programming around self-expression, the ability to express and discern truth, and the expression of being who you wish to be. If this chakra is imbalanced or blocked, it can cause fear of expressing your truth, a lack of confidence in expressing your points and views, inconsistency in what you say and do, social anxiety, and a fear of speaking. It can also cause arrogance, domination manipulation, and excessive eating.

The throat chakra is linked to the neck, jaw, nose, teeth, thyroid, ears. If you are suffering from issues in these areas, it is highly likely that there is an imbalance, and healing is to be done. When the throat chakra is balanced, you can express your thoughts and inner feelings without shyness or self-judgment, and you will find your actions match your words.

The **Ajna**, also known as the third eye, is responsible for the programming of your direction in life. It allows you to let go of the ego so that you can follow the voice of your soul. It is also what we use to imagine, so it is the tool we have to create our realities. If this chakra is imbalanced or blocked, then it can cause a lack of direction, life purpose, ability to see positive outcomes, faith in intuition, and belief in inner wisdom.

This chakra is linked with the pituitary gland and neurological functions. If you find yourself suffering from poor vision, migraines, delusions, seizures, and constant nightmares, then it is highly likely there is healing to be done here. A healthy functioning third eye produces feelings of being to take things in stride, knowing what you want from life, and trusting that you know how to get there.

The **Sahasrara**, also known as the crown chakra, is responsible for the programming around your connection to the Divine, your spiritualism, and your link to universal knowledge. If this chakra is imbalanced or blocked, it can create feelings of disconnectedness to others, a lack of life direction, the inability to set and maintain goals, and feelings of being disconnected spiritually.

This chakra is linked with brain and neurological functions. If you find yourself suffering from nerve pain, insomnia, depression, reoccurring headaches, or neurological disorders, then it is highly possible that healing is to be done in this area.

Those are the seven basic chakras and their functions. It is easy to see how so many people are out of harmony with themselves.

Although we all have these chakra energy centers, most people haven't even activated these centers due to the system's attempt to distort the truth about them. Going back to the CD and CD player analogy, although the disk has the tracks on it (that is, programming installed), most players are just running track after track, including those songs we don't like or enjoy (beliefs and programs). But the great news is that these discs are rewriteable. When we acknowledge these centers and activate them, we can start to remove certain tracks we don't enjoy and replace them with ones we do, thereby bringing new health and well-being to the soul.

Our physical and mental health issues do not just start as physical only but are mental. Everything starts in the mind, the aura of the human body. That aching shoulder isn't just a physical ache but an energetic blockage within the mental body—chakra centers.

All health and mental issues start with negative thoughts. The persistence of those negative mental thoughts and beliefs held within the mind and chakras eventually manifest in the physical body. Thoughts of stress or money worries will create that aching shoulder. That is why those pills you have been told to take do nothing but mask the pain. Once you stop taking them, that same pain come back.

Once we start to understand that our physical issues are caused by more than physical issues, we can heal them using the power of thought by activating and reprogramming o the chakras centers.

Did you know that the human body is completely renewed every seven years? Yes, every seven years, we have the chance to heal all our issues.

It all starts with you. Activate, heal, and balance those chakra centers and strengthen the programming with positive thoughts. Change those thoughts to ones of positivity and vibrancy. Science has already proven that our bodies react to our thoughts. Every cell has its own intelligence that mirrors the mind and spirit. There is plenty of information out there on this and many other subjects we've discussed.

Science has proven that the body and its cells react to thoughts. The more positive the thought, the more freely the blood flows, the healthier the skin and the building blocks of the cells. The same can also be said for negativity. Negative thoughts caused the blood not to flow as fluently and easily. Your cells feel the stress of your thoughts, showing up as bad skin, mental issues, reduced sight, and muffled hearing.

Using the universal law of attraction, visualize how you wish to be, how you wish to look, AND how you wish to feel physically, emotionally, and mentally. What does this look like? How do you feel l with this positive self-image of mind, body, and spirit?

When creating through visualization, always include as much detail as you can. As Albert Einstein said, "What the mind can conceive, it can achieve." Feel it. See it. Touch it. Form the picture in full detail as best you can—how you look and feel, how others see you, how you wish to be seen, your weight, skin tone, etc.

Remember this: believe you are that you wish to be, and you will co-create with the Universe that which you wish to be. Hence the expression, "Fake it until you make it." By changing your thoughts, words, and actions, you will begin to create health within you and around you.

Through a balance of healthy thoughts about yourself your body, and your soul, your body will begin to heal. Remember, health creates health, so you may find that you start to change your diet to a more resonate, higher frequency diet. Old habits may no longer appeal to you, health issues conditions may improve or even miraculously disappear, vitality may improve, the way you hold yourself and present yourself may change, and the way you speak and communicate may change. These changes are but a few of the main ones you may start to notice as you shape your new reality by re-programming your core beliefs.

We can also use our angels and guides here by invoking them to come to us to help heal any false beliefs and remove any blockages in the body that are causing us to evade the life of our dreams, the love we desire, and the abundance waiting to be given to us. As I have previously mentioned, there are many angels, elementals, and ascended masters who all specialize in many areas. They can help with removing blockages in the aura (chakras) and cutting energy cords (karma), which we will talk about later. They can help with cleansing your aura and turning those negative self-thoughts into positive ones.

To bring into a state of conscious health, we need to focus not only on the physical aspects but also on the mental body. Remember that our health issues and illness might be coming from more than this life. You may be bringing over karmic energy from a past life or created a soul experience to gain a better understanding of that which you never fully understood in a previous life. Therefore, rather than opting for traditional healing methods, it may be best to try soul healing methods: in-between life sessions, past life regression, and soul retrieval.

What is soul retrieval?

As we know, souls live many lives and have had many experiences. They can and do leave a part of themselves in certain moments. This detachment or disassociation as it is known in the medical industry mainly happens in experiences of pain, trauma, hard relationships, or hard times as a child. We try to avoid these experiences, so if they do happen, it helps to remove ourselves consciously from the experience.

What happens is a part of the soul detaches itself and stays in the moment. This detachment can cause you to be unable to forgive or overcome such experiences as on a soul level part of you is still living out the moment, this if not healed or called back to you can be the cause of mental and physical illnesses, But by going into meditation or with the help of a soul therapist or hypnotherapist, you can call back those aspects of the soul. This process is called "soul retrieval."

Of course, it is not as easy as saying, "Come back." you must be ready to forgive and send love to that experience—to yourself and all included. By doing so, you are showing the soul that you have understood the purpose of those experiences. Then and only then can you call back those lost aspects.

Again, it's all about love and forgiveness of the self and others. When you see from the high-vibration perspective, you will be able to call back all the lost parts of the soul, which can bring a dramatic healing experience.

Soul retrieval is just one of the many soul healing methods available to us, but the main method we can use to completely overcome trauma. There are many forms of alternative healing available to help us, such as reiki, crystal healing, chakra cleansing, past life regressions, acupuncture, and cupping, just to name a few. But again, due to the distortion of mass media, most people are not aware of these alternatives—not to mention that most don't believe these healing methods can heal.

Those who have sought to control humanity have created false opinions by mocking and ridiculing those who speak in favor of such healing methods. Why? Because they only care about control and profits. They know that by holding these thoughts, we will go and buy the pills that only make things worse and that we will only create that outcome. It's only through faith and belief in who you truly are that you can heal yourself. Resistance only creates more resistance. Once we start to heal ourselves, we can then show others how to heal and heal the world.

There are many alternative healing methods available to us. Please have a look into these various healing methods and see what resonates with you, if you wish to know more information there is plenty resources both on the internet and in books.

The Message about Food, Health, and Exercise

Many healing techniques have been purposely kept from us. This is our time to bring forth these techniques and embrace them as the full healing power they are, including the power of healing through plants and foods.

Health isn't just about physical appearance but mainly about the health of the thoughts you think. Healthy thoughts create healthy bodies, negative thoughts create unhealthy bodies, this science has proven.

Many of the health issues humanity faces is simply due to the forgetting of who we are and the ability to heal ourselves without the need for prescriptions or pills. These just mask the symptoms but never cure the root of the cause.

Many health issues stem from unhealthy thoughts, but also energic blockages within the body energy system (aura), which come from various reasons such as repression of emotional expression, what we may have experience and taken in board as a self-belief, but more often than not stem from a lack of self-love and worth of one self.

Chakras are energy systems placed within the body which is like a disk that holds your core beliefs in accordance with the subject matters it is associated with. Health issues can be better understood by understanding the chakra system and the part it plays in the physical experience.

What we think we become, science has proven that thoughts effect the body and its appearance, changing food diets alone won't heal those deeper health issues.

For all diseases and illnesses in the world, there is a natural cure, if it's not using the power of the divine mind then it will come from a source of nature often some form of plant.

Health issues aren't always as clear cut as they may seem, most health issues arise to make us aware of an imbalance within the mind, imbalances within the mind create imbalances with the body (as above so below) so before taking the pills or prescriptions as yourself "what is this showing me?" this is taking responsibility of your health.

Physical looks show us only what we think we see, a mirror does reflect your true image but the image you hold of yourself, so if you want to feel love, and been seen as pretty then you must hold these thoughts of yourself within your consciousness. What we think we become; what we think, we see.

Modern medicine does its best to heal us but ultimately it is business, business need customers to make money so the truth is the powers that be don't want to fully heal you, this is why the soul is saying it is up to you to take responsibility for your health and healing.

Make it your responsibility to be aware of your thought patterns, to be aware of what energies you place yourself around and also what you put in your body.

There are many alternative healing methods which produce better results, this method deals with getting to the root of the issue rather than masking it. By doing this you are also re-claiming your power.

As you become more aware and awakened to your divine nature you will find that diet and lifestyle will naturally change and become more aligned with your new energy frequency.

The Media and Governments

Although television has been around since 1888, it wasn't until 1927 when Philo Taylor Farnsworth created the first all-electronic television system that TVs became mass-produced and used around the world. Although it was a breakthrough in innovation, Farnsworth was even rumored to have said to his son, "TV is a waste of life, time and served no purpose." He banned TVs from his own home, saying the moment he invented it, he "regretted it."

In this chapter, I will discuss why war, destruction, and fear-based news, media, propaganda is always pushed upon us, why computer games are mainly focused on war, fighting, and survival, and why we have TV programs and movies encouraging low vibrational living and mental states. All these things are teaching us and trying to distort our moral compasses and family values. I'll also talk about why we are furiously bombarded with endless consumer messages (both consciously and subconsciously) through many different forms of advertising, their overall consciousness purpose, how these factors combined have created the fear-based world we see today, and how we are separated by being subconsciously forced to excessively compete rather than collaborate.

The world we see today is ruled and dominated by the few (the global elites) who own and use all mainstream media outlets to form negative public opinion, create addictions, and manipulate our consciousness. This work creates more fear, which in turn creates more separation, giving the global elites power.

I find it funny when people talk about the pending WWIII. What people don't understand is that it has already begun and has been going on since time began. The war is the war on consciousness.

Let's start with the media and its impacts on society. But before I begin, I want to make it clear that I am not saying that *all* media is out to control us. There are many TV shows and broadcasts that promote good vibrations, were created for pure entertainment, and to focus on personal self-development. For example, the website Gaia.com is a great site and media outlet that promotes soul growth and spiritual development. There are many other higher consciousness media outlets too.

The focus of this chapter is on mainstream media, highlighting the ways the global elites and these mainstream corporations and governments manipulate human consciousness through subliminal messages, symbolism, and false propaganda. The reason for this mind control—or conscious control, as I like to call it—is to ensure that we don't think for ourselves and to keep us in a low vibration consciousness level so that we keep turning to the media to solve our every issue and so that we fight to keep the status quo. They want us in a low vibrational state because it keeps us from raising our vibrations and becoming aware of who we are and our Divine gifts. It keeps the global elites in control by having us "freely" hand over our Divine power. It keeps the global elites in power.

The global elites need us to be in a low vibrational state to keep the status quo. Those who seek to control the masses thrive off fear and use that fear to create that which they wish to see in the world.

The global elites know the truth about the Universe. They know that we create and the power of thought. Therefore, mainstream news channels and media are doing the work for the global elites, which promotes fear, ego, negative public opinion, competition, hate, separation, and lower vibration mental states. Its why they create fake wars and so-called terrorist attacks. These so-called terrorists are, in fact, part of the bigger agenda and part of the organizations working for these governments that we believe here to protect us.

Remember, we are all creators of that which we experience. The same can be said for the collective experience. One mind creating is powerful, but two minds creating is extra powerful. Can you imagine all the minds of the world collectively creating and our power and energy combined? It's a power that we can't even begin to fathom, a power that could move mountains and part the seas. If we were to become aware of the power of the collective consciousness, then we would no longer sit in front of a box (the TV) listening to what it is telling us to be, do, and feel. We would no longer buy magazines and newspapers full of false news and that only produce negativity. But of because this is not what the powers that be want for us.

People strongly believe that TV is here to help us, teach us, and entertain us. While that belief this is partly true, it is not the purpose of mainstream programming.

The TV is not your friend. It doesn't want you to love who you are or love others. It doesn't want to teach you positive things, to be your own person, or to think for yourself, and it most certainly doesn't want you to remember who you truly are.

When you look at mainstream TV from this perspective, you will see the real agenda behind this programming. Seeing TV from this perspective will enable you to enjoy the entertainment aspects while removing yourself from the attempts of false programming upon your subconscious.

One clue is in the name: television programming. "Program" as in "to program you."

Let's define the word "program." There are many different definitions of the word "program," and that is no accident. These multiple definitions were created to give us a false idea about what is truly going on. We find this a lot in the English language. One word with on hundred meanings. This situation serves to create more confusion and mental manipulation.

Regardless of the other hundreds of meanings, the definition of "program" we are focusing on is this perspective meaning "to tell a device or system to operate in a particular way, or part a particular time." This definition is the truth the agenda is when it comes to TV, magazines, and radio, for that matter. They are there to program you, to program your subconscious (the system) regarding what is right and wrong, what is good and bad, what to feel and when to feel it (operate in a particular way), and how to perceive yourself, people, and the world. You are subconsciously being programmed to be how the global elite wants you to be, and they do this by creating mass public opinion and corporate profits.

The media's new agenda seems to be to distort your moral compass and family values. Take soap operas for instance, the main theme of these shows are affairs, death and disease. Just take a minute and think about that, how TV or media have caused you judge and label things and people.

How many times have you read something or watched something that has created a certain feeling to rise within you? How many times has the media has persuaded you to buy a certain thing or told you to judge something in a certain way? How many times has it told you and created your "truth" for you?

Just to put in perspective the idea I'm getting at here, try this scenario

Just take a minute to think of a stereotypical image, such as that of a homeless person. Put that in your mind. Now ask yourself where you got those ideas of what a homeless person looks like from, and the reason they could be homeless. Chances are they are opinions formed from watching TV or reading a magazine.

Try this one, think of what is known to be fashionable whether a top or a piece of jewelry, now ask where you got the idea that this item was deemed as fashionable, you see when you think you start to realize that many of the ideals and beliefs you believe are truly yours are in fact someone's, who have through subliminal means have tricked you into believe their truth, which in turn made it your truth.

Did you know that when the patent for the TV was issued, scientists did some research on its effects on the watcher? This is what they found:

> **Physiological effects have been observed in a human subject in response to stimulation of the skin with weak electromagnetic fields that are pulsed with certain frequencies near ½ Hz or 2.4 Hz, such as to excite a sensory resonance. Many computers monitor's and TV tubes, when displaying pulsed images, emit pulsed electromagnetic fields of sufficient amplitudes to cause such excitation. It is therefore possible to manipulate the nervous system of a subject by pulsing images displayed on a nearby computer monitor or TV set.[4]**

There is much more they say on this topic, but I want to focus on the statement, "It is therefore possible to manipulate the nervous system of a subject by pulsing images displayed on a nearby computer monitor or TV set." The media can not only implant ideas through the images on a TV screen but also affect the viewer's emotions natural bodily functions.

The global elites know that if we all put our energy into a cause created by them, then we will create that very cause ourselves. Therefore, they create endless fake wars, terrorist attacks, and other false flag events that they promote through TV. They know that these energies, events, and experiences can only be created by us for their gain and agenda, but only if we give them our energy and permission.

---

[4]. "Nervous System Manipulation by Electromagnetic Fields from Monitors," Google Patents, https://patents.google.com/patent/US6506148B2/en.

Again, we are going back to the law of free will. Nothing in the universe can harm us or take or use our energy useless we give it permission to do so. If we didn't give our conscious energy to the things we see on mainstream media, the corporations and governments would simply hold no power. The only way the global elites can bring these energies and experiences into fruition is by using our collective creative energy against us to create that which they wish to see, which is exactly what they do. But why?

There are more of us than them, so they want to prevent an uprising, so to speak. That is why the global elites try to convince us that endless wars are going on. They want to control the whole world, and to do so, we must give permission. The only way they can get us to give them permission is to make it seems like we need them to be safe and survive.

This propaganda is all an attempt to keep us in survival mode so that we don't raise our vibrations and start to bring forth new energies of Divine love and unite. They know that unity creates power, which would overthrow their plans.

What we have forgotten is that every emotional reaction and word spoken adds energy to the cause, each person causing that certain thing or energy to gain momentum. With all creative processes, enough energy given to the cause will create it to happen in the physical.

How can we stop recreating these low vibrational events? How can we stop the global elites? It's simple. Don't give them your energy. Don't get sucked into the distortion and lies of the media. Don't do, as they say.

Don't be who they wish you to be. Be that which you are! That which you were born to be! Bring in those divine vibrations and say goodbye to the global elites for good. Only when we stop getting sucked into the TV, papers, and all things external and focus on the internal will we change the outcome. It simply takes a change of thought and redirected focus.

It is the same process we use to create for ourselves. That which we focus energy on and pay attention to will manifest. Whenever there is a so-called terrorist attack or event and we react to it, we are contributing to creating that very same energy, which will inevitably create a similar event.

Remember, like attracts like, and like creates like. Negative thoughts and feelings around terrorists create only create more energies of terrorism, and the experience of that energy is eventually in a physical form (a terrorist attack). Just like how persistent negative thoughts create illnesses and diseases in the body, the same can be applied here.

The same intention can be said for the entertainment and retail industry. They tell us how we should dress, what we should think, what is good and bad, and what to believe we are and must be. They subconsciously creating insecurities and false beliefs, forming public opinion.

Due to this endless bombardment of an all-consuming war waged against our minds, bodies, and spirits, we now have more methods of self-destruction, more mental issues, more insecurities, more fear, more wars, more famine, and more poverty than ever. The global elites predominately use lowered frequencies, vocal undertones, and symbolism for subliminal messages.

What is a subliminal message? A subliminal message is an auditory or visual affirmation or message that is presented below the normal limits of human auditory or visual perception.

There are many triggers and subliminal messages hidden within computer games, music, and advisements. These messages can include emotional reactional symbols, what we should fear, how we should perceive others, how we should think, and how we should feel about ourselves and others. They are also used to implant scenario ideas.

Through repetitive images, the powers that be can program how you react in a certain situation. Ever wondered why many films are released all at once with the same undertone? Right now, they're all end-of-the-world and alien-invasion films. This mas release is simply to program how you react in these situations.

The same awareness can be applied to the music and radio industry. Yes, the global elites have infiltrated these channels, too, and use them again to control us, steal our creative consciousness energy, form public opinion, and implant pro-programming.

Scientists have done experiments with water to see if certain sounds and vibrations have an effect, and the results were remarkable.

It is estimated that the human body is made up of 70% water. That would mean that if certain vibrations have a negative effect on water, then those same vibrations would and do have a negative effect on our bodies and consciousness.

There was an experiment originally undertook by Dr. Masaru Emoto and repeated by many others whereby in this experiment, a certain word was placed upon a container of water, and then the container was frozen. Some words were positive, and some were negative. The results are just mind-blowing. Due to copy right I haven't included the images of the outcomes that these words had on the crystalized water particles but if you go on the internet you can find many images which show what I am talking of here,

The results from various experiments found that the positive words and thoughts, such as "thank you," "please," and "I love you," created beautiful symmetrical crystalline formations. However, when the water as subjected to negative words and thoughts, such as "fool," "war," and "I hate you," the formations created distorted, less symmetrical patterns, often looking very unpleasant. The same experiment was done with rice, and the outcome was identical. The rice placed in a jar with a positive stayed almost fresh and fermented, whereas the rice placed in a jar with a negative word went black and smelt awful.

The reason I have mentioned this experiment is that the music we subject ourselves to has more of an effect on us than we realize. Most mainstream music is recorded at a frequency lower than 440 Hz, which has been said to be disharmonic to the body. Mainstream music uses this frequency in its recordings and often speaks of negativity in a way that we are oblivious to. We often find that the music is catchy and upbeat but with lyrics are of a lower vibrational tone or vice versa. Songs are often about sexual domination, war, hate, separation, revenge, judgment, fear, and fear-based love. These topics are chosen on purpose to get you to resonate at these levels of frequencies and, thus, create these negative thoughts within your subconscious.

It has been documented that when music is recorded and played at the frequency of 432 Hz, it is more harmonic to the body than at 440 Hz. This frequency is close to the frequency of the human heart.

When you look at the geometric structure of the water's reaction to sound played at 432 Hz you will find it frequency sound pattern is more symmetrical, while the geometric structure of the water's reaction to sound played at 440 Hz (the frequency of mainstream music) is less flowing, less spacious, and less symmetrical. Just imagine what is happening to your body after constantly putting it in a vibration of 440 Hz. Again, these images can be found on the internet.

Let's move on to the effect and agenda of subliminal messages, vocal undertones, and symbolism. We'll expand on them to give you a better understanding and awareness of what they are and what they mean.

Subliminal messaging has been used by the global elites since time began to keep us in a low vibrational state. They do so through repetition. We associated certain symbols with a certain emotion. Subliminal messages aim emotionally trigger us, and they are used not only subliminally but also through media outlets.

Much of what is seen on TV and in magazines is set to create an emotional response. This emotional response is the creative energy or driving force behind the creation of much of the world we see today. TV and media have only one use: to produce an emotional reaction. While you give your energy to the negative events shown in the media (which have basically been made up), others can use their energy to create these events to benefit the powers that be. They prevent or distract you from using that same emotional or creative energy to create that which you wish to see in your reality and, even more so, distract you from uncovering who you truly are, finding your happiness, and feeling your joy and peace. The media does this work by triggering a change in emotional states, and they are doing without you even knowing or being aware of it. It's this emotional hijacking that creates all sorts of problems in the individual and collective consciousness.

The global elites want to replace positive vibrations with negative vibrations. They take symbols of peace and high vibration and invert them to invert the vibration. Take, for example, the classic is the Buddhist peace sign, which was later termed the swastika.

The Buddhist swastika was a sign of peace recognized by Buddhists as the path of the Buddha according to the Buddhist religion. Just like with everything that was meant to be a positive symbol, they distorted it and tarnished to bring down its high vibration and lower its meaning by associating it with the Nazi's and creating a new but distorted meaning for that sign.

The swastika is not the only symbol whose meaning has been distorted. Throughout history, the global elites have stripped symbols of their higher vibrational and positive meanings. They have done it with every symbol you can think of. Another example is the peace sign. This symbol was also distorted to produce the opposite effect than it used to have.

The peace sign is not the downwards symbol we all think it is and recognize. In fact, it's supposed to be upwards (Figure 2). The original peace sign represented the tree of life and promoted positive energy.

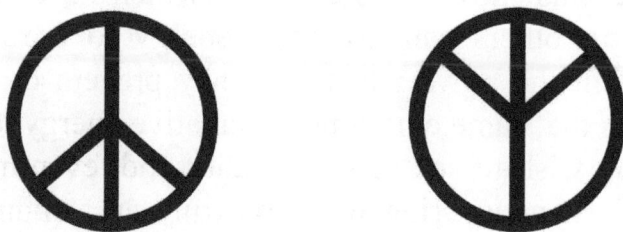

Figure 4. The peace sign as we know it (left) and the original peace sign (right).

The most common explanation for the peace symbol as we know it was written by Gerald Holtom (the man who supposedly created this peace sign). According to sources on Wikipedia He claims that he created it in 1958 and used to represent the link between the end of nuclear weapons and the beginning of peace. The combined symbol was enclosed in a circle to represent the "all-encompassing" or "total." Holtom is supposed to have said that he was in despair when creating the symbol.

That the image of the man was actually himself and represented his individual despair, with hands palm outstretched outwards and downwards in the manner of Goya's peasant before the firing squad. He then formalized the drawing into a line and put a circle round it.

It was said that Holtom even asked for the upright symbol to be placed on his grave. Which if you look up images of his grave you will see that the request was ignored. (image can be seen on google images)

According to sources on the internet the peace symbol also dates back to ancient times. Nero, who is remembered for persecuting Christians.

"Nero was said to be so wicked that he even had his mother executed. The First Roman-Jewish War (66–70 AD) started during his reign. Today, the Nero cross (found in today's peace symbol) is the symbol of the "broken Jew" or the "broken cross." It was used for centuries and was adapted into satanic rituals". The Nero cross was used during World War II by Hitler's third panzer division (tanks) from 1941 to 1945. [5]

The way the global elites ultimately distort positive symbols is to place them in energies of war or fear, which is why they can always be found in government places, such as on army uniforms, military vehicles, and aircraft.

The pentagram (Figure 5) is another distorted symbol. The symbol was once well known as a symbol of protection, mainly energy protection. It is another positive symbol that the global elites have distorted and tarnished by saying it's the symbol of the devil and using it in satanic rituals.

---

[5] Taken from https://www.kehrey.com/peace-sign-history.html

Figure 5. The pentagram.

Creating a relationship between symbols and signs of positivity and peace and a high vibration with war, violence, or the so-called devil is a common occurrence. Of course, whenever we think of the devil (fear), we think of hell, which produces low vibrational thoughts and feelings of fear. That is simply the intention behind this agenda. The main agenda with these symbols is to project a low sub consciousness vibration, which has been created by manipulating positive symbols into negative icons through eons of symbolism programming.

Subliminal undertones are basically messages hidden within a film or song. They can be found when a certain song is played backward, in low binaural frequencies, or when you simply listen closer. We think that we have control over what influences us, over what we take in and what we don't. But the truth is our subconscious takes everything in, whether we are aware or not. The subconscious is very intelligent and can decipher these messages. That is the reason for all the satanic or fear-based symbolism within the mainstream music videos, album imagery, films, and TV programs, and even children's programs. The earlier they can instill this symbolic energy programming, the more effective the hold they have over us, and the easier we are to manipulate and control.

This same awareness and agenda are found in gaming and consoles. Yes, video games are fun and can promote learning, but the global elites' main intention is to use them to dumb us down and create military personnel. Notice how most video games are about survival or war. It is a fact that private companies such as the CIA and NSA sponsor many of the games released and have a say about what is added and what is not. Therefore, they can glorify themselves if they need too. They are subconsciously trying to create fighters so that we fight for the very system that keeps us enslaved. They promote war and killing, making it look like it's fun, again distorting that inner moral compass and affecting our ability to feel empathy. Most kids these days find these video games fun and don't think twice about rolling around a map and killing innocent animals or people. It is not their fault. We learn from what we observed and what we're told.

The global elites are using these video games to demoralize our human nature and our natural senses. They make it seem like killing is something to honor (if we are on the winning side) when, in fact, there is no honor in war. The global elites just want use to fight their made-up wars. We put our lives on the line to help them keep the status quo, handing over our power mentally, physically, and spiritually.

By keeping us chained to the TV, computers, consoles, and everything but ourselves, the global elites can control the information we absorb and the amount we feel. Their goal is to desensitize and dumb humankind down so that we don't ask questions.

I'm not saying that every band, artist, game, or movie is set out to negatively impact our consciousness. There are many games, artists, musicians, and movies out there by independent producers that promote love, compassion, unity, and Divine love, as well as speak of subjects like those in this book. My main point is that we must be aware of the agenda that is in place to control us and manipulate our moral compasses and creative consciousness.

Once you become aware of the subconscious impact of music, computer games, advertisements, radio, TV, and any other form of media, you can start to protect yourself and take your power back. Once you see with Divine eyes the true agenda of the government and mainstream media and entertainment, you can start to refocus your conscious energy on that which you wish to create rather than creating for the global elites.

Everything we discussed regarding the intentions and agenda of the music, entertainment, and media industries is also true for governments.

Governments are nonphysical entities. They hold no power over us other than the power we give them and agree to hand over to them. But because of the idea of placing physicality into the mix, we now have buildings that we deem government buildings and people we call politicians, which has manipulated us into believing that this government is real and that we have a voice.

All the people and buildings are there to trick us into believing that governments are a physical thing. Ask yourself this: Would you really do what a nonphysical entity demands when it is against your Divine will? Would you pay your taxes, which don't go to making the world a better place but go to the research and development of military weapons for more global domination or fund more police on the streets to create even more fear within and without? Would you work a job that damn near kills you and brings you no joy? Would you send your children to fight and die for causes you know nothing about? If those demanding these things of you had no true power and couldn't punish you if you didn't succumb to their demands, would you?

Governments use fear to keep us in check—or the illusion of fear, I should say.

Governments were created to set in place the agenda of the global elites—to put the plans into action but without the true leaders being seen or known. They are the puppets of the system, having their strings pulled. They are used to create illusions of terrorism, war, separation of nations, and separation of people, and debt. They incite fear into the consciousness of the world, which causes us to unknowingly hand over our creative power and prevents us from creating for ourselves. Those in power revel in us being in the fear vibration because by being in a state of fear, we enable and increase their creative power.

It's not the politicians who are setting the policies and budgets. (Money is energy, and energy is infinite, so there technically is no budget. Everything is in abundance, so it is an illusion.) It's the shadow government or the string-pullers: the bankers and corporations.

Whenever there is an election, the winner is always the person the majority didn't vote for. Why? Because we don't have a say. We don't matter to the global elites. Only their power, control, and agenda matters, and they will do anything it takes to set in play this agenda. Aaron Russo a humanitarian once said that when it comes to those who wish to control, who feel we are not responsible enough to look after ourselves and make our own choices, they truly believe that "the ends justify the means." Despite what promises may be made or what words are spoken, they will always do what benefits their agenda, not the masses.

The global elites always chose who is going to be in power. After all, in this realm, power comes from money, and money always comes from the same source. Those who are placed in high positions have been allowed to be there, or else the powers that be would have their reputation tarnished by creating false stories pushed out through again mainstream media or simply have them silenced. This fear is the reason why many whistle-blowers or informers who have tried to come forth with this information have been prevented from doing so.

So how do we take our power back? It's simple. Remove yourself from the persistent programming and false icons of the TV by cutting out or down the hours you spend watching it and eliminate all mainstream news—the global elites' main source of consciousness manipulation. These mediums are all designed to distract us from the real issues going on in and around us, create fear in ourselves, create negative public opinion, and persuade us to buy, buy, buy so we that we get into debt, debt, debt. They do all this while also causing competition (separation between people and nations)—who's got the latest gadgets, what wealth, health, and success look like— so that we hand over our creative consciousness to those who wish to use it against us.

Don't look to governments to govern you. Govern yourself, your thoughts, your healing, and your creations. Come together with like-minded souls and simply be the change you wish to see.

I'm not saying to become an introvert and retreat from society. Rather, simply take a step back from that which you're attached to—in this instance, emotionally attached to—and focus on your being through meditation, writing, adventures in nature, and self-development. By doing so, we can diminish the effects of the campaigns and programming unknowingly set upon us. Through cultivated awareness of the bigger picture of the war on consciousness, we have the power to dissolve the global elites' agendas and missions of mind control and, eventually, all of their control.

It is about the willingness to consciously dedicate time to uncover Divine knowledge of the Universal processes (Universal laws) and of the self, to pay attention to personal problems and creations, such as self-healing, mental processes, and to direct your energy in a way that serves you and the world. You can call on the angels and ascended masters to help and support you in every way, in all your endeavors. Simply being aware of the true agenda gives you all the power you need to take yours back.

We must not send hate or resent the governments. Negative energy only creates negative energy, and that which we resist, persists. Therefore, despite the governments' deeper agenda, we must send love and forgiveness. It may be hard to do, but just like everything else in this reality, only love can cure.

By sending love, we place a new energy in those positions and, thus, stop the recreation of past energies. By holding energies of hate, anger, and resentment, we only increase the power and hold the global elites have over us. But by holding a positive vision of a government that looks after the people's needs and is there to bring unity and balance to all, we will create it. Again, its belief made manifest.

Remember how the global elites use media as a way to get us to use our creative energy to create false wars for their agenda? Well, we can use our Divine love energy to heal the government. In the same way that they use our energies against us, we can use our energies *for* them. They use our powers against us because there are more of us, so we technically hold more power than they ever could. Let's use that energy not to hate or resent but to bless and heal. By doing so, we will create a new foundation on which the government will be built upon while destroying the old ways, and all with the power of love and the vision of a positive outcome for all. The imagination holds more power than most can comprehend.

The Message about the Media and Governments

Media has a powerful impact on the opinions of humankind. While not all media is meant to brainwash us, most TV and media outlets are trying to push the global elites' agenda and promote fear and separation. Be aware of the truth of media and its objectives. By being aware, you will take your power back from external influences.

Balance is key. You don't have to stop playing video games or watching films. Just simply be aware of the message and bring in balance. Take time to watch mind-expanding documentaries in amongst the soaps and reality TV. Listen to higher vibrational music among the lower mainstream music frequencies. Mix walks and hikes with the cyber world—remember, the outdoors is critical to your balancing of mind, body, and spirit.

Take time to be nice to yourself. With everyone telling you that it's wrong to love yourself, take the time to talk to your self nicely. Listen to positive affirmations and write down what you like about yourself. Reconnect with the love of your being.

Don't believe everything that is shown to you on TV and in the media. Remember that these outlets are controlled by the same people who wish to keep us enslaved.

Finally, take responsibility for what you expose your mind, body, and spirit to.

Lifestyles, Corporations, and World Resources

I have already spoken about how we can improve our health through consciousness, how we are made to live in fear of judgment of who we are and what we look like, and the true agendas of governments. In this chapter, I want to focus on our lifestyle and how we can change it not just for the individual but for the collective, how we can see all of the world as a place of safety, peace, prosperity, and abundance.

Governments are set up by the global elites to benefit themselves and a select few major corporations, which are owned by the same global elites. I'm not saying that they haven't helped progress humanity, because, in many ways, they have. But they have mainly used these outlets to continue to control and dominate us and our way of living. They have continually backed the falsely created wars we get shown through media to gain access to more of the world's resources, and they have continually kept us from believing in the power we hold so that we hand it over to them. If we knew the truth of the power, we each have, we would no longer find any use for governments.

Governments and corporations serve the same purpose: to take away the power of the individual and use it against them. That is why many local farms and food stores have closed down and why farmers are struggling to grow crops. These large corporations have made it so hard for these independent businesses to make a profit due to genetically modified foods and large-scale industrial production of foods—not to mention the agenda to ruin topsoil through chemical air trails.

We have been so brainwashed by the government and corporations that we believe they are here to help us, to provide us with what we need. On the one hand, that is true. But they mostly just want to make huge profits, which again is due to power and control.

The main reason paper money was created was to fool us into believing we could only have that thing we want if we pay for it—if we have physical cash to hand over. That is just not true. Everything in the material world is but energy. Energy attracts like energy, so by creating a system in which the global elites have fooled us into believing that there isn't enough or that we don't have the right to have what we want, we have created that illusion for ourselves. We have the power to create nothing in the physical.

Through fear-based thinking, the global elites have gained control of every aspect of our lives, and we just go along with it. Just think, if we didn't judge each other on looks and the physical alone, we wouldn't have such things as makeup and cosmetics. These industries were created out of the fear of not living up to society's standards of physical appearance and are used in this day and age to continually push mental insecurities around what is aesthetically beautiful and acceptable. The global elites have literally turned us against one another by forming these public opinions so that they can control and make profits off us.

This work has mainly been done with women, but these days, the global elites have started manipulating men in the same way. Governments and corporations tell us how we should live our lives, causing us to compete against one another. They tell people how to look and what to wear promoting the use of makeup and multiple cosmetic products.

We get told these products will help us be happy or to help with our health and well-being when, in fact, the products we buy and put on our bodies cause bodily harm in the long run.

I'm not saying one should not have implants or change themselves cosmetically. Again, that is up to the soul. I am simply saying that we should not be making these changes because of the judgment and fear placed upon us.

Most products, from food and cosmetics to DIY, are all owned by a small group of major corporations. They make it look like there are many of them to fool us and so that we don't ask the questions, "Why do all the resources in the world belong to the few?" and "Why does all the money in the world go to the same families?" This goes back to the fact if we knew the truth about corporations, we wouldn't invest in them, they wouldn't make profits, and they would lose the power to control us. Their goal is simply to make money and control us.

We have allowed all of the world's resources to be owned by the few. That is the system the global elites have created, and we allowed it to happen by continually giving power to them and by turning against one another, judging one another on what they look like, have, or live like.

The global elites own the food, health, energy, electric, oil, motor, and travel industries— you name it, they own it. Even the governments and such things are the police, CIA, are justice system are all owned by privately owned businesses. They are privately owned because they don't want you to know who they are, so they hide behind corporations, sub-businesses, and other illusions. But there is always a person at the top who makes the rules.

Many companies are all owned by a select few who you can guarantee work in or for the families of the global elites and serve their agenda for complete domination and control o. After all, these companies make money, so if a business becomes that large, it's because the global elites have let it.

All the big brands in the world are owned by a handful of corporations. Whether its food, cleaning products, banks, airlines, cars, media, or telecoms companies, everything is in the hands of these mega-corporations, and these mega-corporations owned by the 1%

It's time that you see the agenda from a soul perspective, from a higher view. It's only when we see what's truly happening that we can change it. These governments and corporations have molded not only the way we live our lives but also how we judge the standards of the lives we live. They have caused us to compete in our everyday lives, which has caused us to give our power to them. It's time to change this situation. For too long, these governments, banks, corporations, and global elites have enslaved humanity. For too long, we have given our power to these energies. Now is a time of great change. We must take our power back.

How do we do that?

It's simple. Just like with everything else, the global elites need us to comply. They need our energy to manifest their reality. If we do not give it, they will crumble.

I'm not saying we should cause complete anarchy. Rather, we should simply change our focus and work together to create a balance and equal living standards for all. Let's stop buying into these corporations' attempts to create fear and insecurities within us. Let's get back into the heart space, remember the love we are, and share it not with just ourselves but the world. Let's use our energy to remove unfair systems, such as the current benefits system in place in the UK. It causes people more health issues due to stress, and stressed people are just trying to survive.

These systems were created by those who do not live by the rules set by governments. Those rules do not apply to them. Those rules and systems only apply to 99% of humanity that is enslaved. We need to say no and peacefully remove these people from their positions of power. For too long has the older generation kept the chains on humanity, setting rules and putting in place regulations that they themselves do not abide by. This reality is an illusion we must destroy.

Let's say no to unfair councils or housing systems. Let's say no to unfair employment systems, let's say no to these major corporations and start saying yes to us, to the All. We can do this by standing together, by unifying and taking back our power, by using the same power and energy we give to them for ourselves and the world. We can heal homelessness, poverty, and unfairness by not taking part in the system, by standing up for your fellow neighbor. Once we stand together, the global elites lose all their power. That is why they have created a system with so much separation.

How can we change this system and the lifestyle we all experience without causing complete anarchy?

We can use our Divine gifts, our souls, to visualize a new world, a world where no one goes hungry, where no one is homeless, where no one struggles to survive, where no one goes without. Rather than buying into the system, we can use that same energy to create a new system in which not just the 1% benefits and has access to the world's resources but 100% benefit. A system in which all are prosperous, and all are abundant in health, wealth, and happiness.

We simply need to envision a world where everything is in balance. Souls create not just individually but collectively. We need to use our creative energy together. If we did that, the world would change.

It is only when we work together that humanity will come into balance with its Divine essence and its energy of love, which includes abundance, prosperity, safety, and well-being for all of humankind. That is what the soul wants, not just for you but for all soul life on Earth. It wants all life to come back into its remembrance of love and the infinite possibilities it is and create together.

You might be thinking, "But I thought the soul chose its experience, so if it is in an experience of poverty, then it chose that." That is true, but just because a soul chose a certain experience doesn't mean it wants to stay in it forever. It will have that experience only until it aligns with its Divine essence in the physical. Remember, souls come to experience. Once they understand that experience, they move on. Once we see the system for what it is and heal it through love, it too will move on. It will evolve.

The Message on Lifestyles, Corporations and Resources

The message is quite simply this, don't buy into all what the external world is telling you, don't be afraid to be unique to dress different, to act different to see differently.

Don't feel pressured to be what you told to be, true strength and influence comes from having the balls to be you, to stand out and up for what you believe in.

Let's show more love and appreciation for the independent food and clothes stores which are more aligned with positive messages and greener living.

As our consciousness raises its vibration, the lifestyle of that soul will dramatically change, this is normal within the ascension process.

There are plenty of resources for all of us on earth, our lack of believing there isn't creates the experience of their not being enough, through change of thoughts around world resources we can bring about a more balanced resource scale for all.

We don't need to send anger or hate to anything or anyone for the control and societal expectations which has been placed upon us, we need but see it for what it is and send love, again through meditation and visualization.

Education and the Modern Generation

The modern education, system like everything in our everyday lives, is set to create more workers for the system, more slaves to the machine. It is derived from the wonderful world of organized religion and politics, teaching children at a young age to follow social norms and planting the ideas that if you don't, God will punish you. It uses fear as a way to control, much like how the media and organized religion create power through fear.

The truth is the education system does not care for harnessing the talents and unique abilities we all hold, nor does it want us to be that which we wish to be. It cares only for keeping the status quo while creating more soldiers to fight for those in power. That is why we get taught things that do us no good in the "real world." Yes, $x+y+=x^2$ would probably useful if we were all physics, scientists, or mathematicians, but let's be honest. Not all of us want to pursue those careers. Most of us the things taught to us hardly ever get used outside of school—not to mention that we have technology that can do all these things for us with us without having to work anything out.

Just like the media and all other advertisements, modern-day education creates separation, mental insecurities, competition, and forms public opinion on a mass scale, in turn creating robots for the machine.

While technology and everything around us have advanced, we still use the same system of education we used back in the 1950s. Just take a moment to go look at classroom lay outs from the twentieth century, and classrooms from the twenty-first century, many images are available in many resources.

You will see that shockingly we still have the same layout with the same intentions. Ancient institutions with ancient methods being used to this day to manipulate our children and the next generation.

The fact that nothing has changed is not an accident. From the moment you enter the education system, you are being programmed to think how the powers that be want you to think, act how they want you to act, and be how they want you to be. How do they do this? By making you get up at industrial hours, sit in a classroom for eight hours while being told who to be and what to think. They set in place unfair schemes and unfair exams to create competition with one another with little or next to no creativity being expressed. They created false ideas of what success is while causing children of the next generation to feel like they are unsuccessful, creating insecurities with the intention of creating laborers to work in factories or soldiers to go to war to fight for those who wish to control the masses.

Just think back to those school days when we were made to sit in rows, much like working in a factory or standing in a military parade. We are made to put our hands up before we expressed ourselves, saying, "Yes, miss, "no, miss," 'yes, sir," "no, sir." This "education" created the program and believe that we must wait and only speak when we allowed too. We would only get a half-hour or hour for lunch, just like when we enter the nine-to-five working world. We were unknowingly being programmed and set up for the continuation of the system.

Schools don't allow children to be themselves. They tell them who to be and stomp out any form of uniqueness. Remember those times when the teacher was talking about something, and you thought to yourself, "That doesn't make sense." But when you would question it, the teacher either push their beliefs onto you or send out for being troublesome or disruptive. In the education system, there is no room for independent thinking nor uniqueness. The modern curriculum stomps out all independent thinking and replace it with little to no thinking at all.

Success in the eyes of modern society and its education system is regurgitating the same shit that has been replayed repeatedly, thus stopping any form of expression of the self's inner wisdom. Therefore, while the world has progressed, thought and education hasn't. The powers that be don't want us or our children to think for ourselves, nor do they want us to stand on our own two feet and express who we are and what we believe in. If we do, then we are a treat to the system. We might cause others to question what they are being told to think. That is how an uprising begins.

The main reason for the extensive use of computers and technology within the education system is to stomp out independent thinking.

The powers that be are using computers to dumb down our children and the next generation. Computers eliminate all right-side brain activity. The right side is the side that produces creativity, innovation, intuition, imagination, and insight, and these aspects go hand in hand with consciousness, creating, and the essence of your soul.

It is scientifically proven that we use fewer muscles and experience less brain activity—including the ability to remember—when using computers. That is why they say if you really wish to remember something, write it down. Writing uses more muscles and increases brain activity, activating the right side of the brain. The powers that be do not want that. The more they can keep you coming from the left side of the brain, the more easily you can be controlled and manipulated, and the easier it is to distract you from finding out who you truly are and what you are truly doing here.

Figure below shows the functions of the brain. Look how the modern world promotes extensive usage of the left-sided brain while eliminating the right-sided functions.

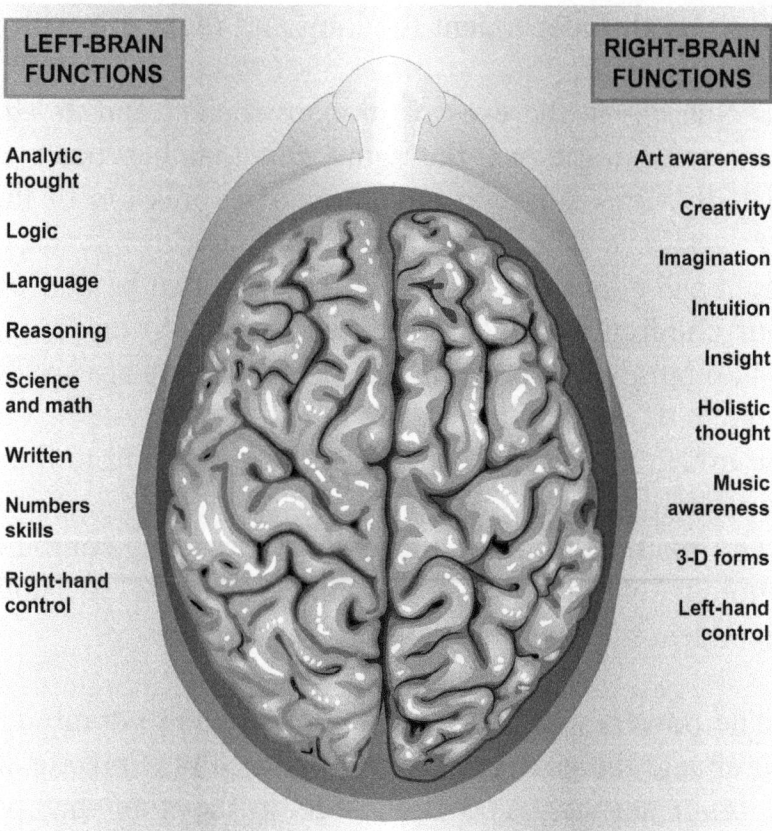

LEFT-BRAIN FUNCTIONS	RIGHT-BRAIN FUNCTIONS
Analytic thought	Art awareness
Logic	Creativity
Language	Imagination
Reasoning	Intuition
Science and math	Insight
Written	Holistic thought
Numbers skills	Music awareness
Right-hand control	3-D forms
	Left-hand control

Figure 6. The functions of the brain.

When you start to see the bigger picture and understand the intentions of the system, then you can start to change it. Change only comes from awareness.

When you compare the education system to the modern-day industrial system, you see that they are identical in their intentions and approach. Why is that? Because that is all the modern schooling system does—create more robots and slaves for the system.

I'm not saying that teachers, principals, and all those working in the education system know this agenda, accept it, and push it. That is simply not true. There are many stories of teachers finding out the truth of the system for themselves. In fact, part of the issue we have is that teachers get paid so little, whereas footballers, singers, and arms personnel all get paid twenty times as much. You can see why there is a lack of people wanting to teach—not to mention to see the system for what it is—and simply can't be a part of it.

There is also the fact that due to the lack of jobs available (or that we are told are available) to people who want to progress in their chosen profession, a lot of people are filling employment spaces in education because that is all there is. This is true not just in education but in all forms of employment. We don't choose the people who fit the job; we choose the people who have the qualifications and paid the money. That's not to say that they aren't suited to the work but that we have been dismissing the fact that many people would be *better* suited to the job who didn't want to spend an extra five to ten years being told how to teach or who didn't have the finances available for them to pursue that career.

Many people are in jobs that do not suit their soul talents, so to speak. They do it for the money, not because of a passion for it. Some feel trapped because they spent so long getting the qualifications only to find that they don't enjoy that particular career. But to change careers would mean that all the time and money spent was a waste of time. This mindset in itself creates problems.

It takes a certain kind of soul to be able to teach while having patience and knowing how to let children express their views. Not all are made for teaching, just like not all are made for engineering or to be doctors, nurses, or soldiers. Each soul has its area of expertise, and we should focus on that, not on how much we can get out of them financially like the system seems to do.

I slightly diverted there, but I felt that that information needed to be brought to our attention because education is the prime factor in the career paths we take. Let's get back on track.

I have a friend who is a supply teacher for second- to sixth grade. One day, I asked him, "What is school like these days?" He responded, "It has really changed. A lot of the schools are becoming academies, causing more competition between students and other academies, and they have now started to bring in military personnel to conduct PE sessions." He said that they were turning physical education to strategic education (a.k.a., army assault courses). I was shocked to hear this. Yes, I had seen and heard a lot about this change, but this was the first time I had heard it from a teacher.

Another one of my experiences that showed evidence of this agenda happened a little over ten years ago. As part of my IT apprenticeship, I took a course in which the students had to sit in front of a screen for eight hours and read page after page with little to no practical experience. I found it hard to keep my concentration and focus. As each week passed, my enthusiasm dwindled, and my passion faded. I nearly got to the point where I was going to leave, because we were just made to sit in one place staring at a screen for hours a day. Now, this type, of course, would be okay if you were the type of person who learns by reading, I am a hands-on person. I learn better by getting physically involved.

The fact that we all learn differently is a major problem we face with education. We are all different, and we all learn in different ways. One size doesn't fit all, so to speak. What we need to do is assess what ways of learning work for each learning type and tailor each course to the students' learning methods rather than trying to fit everyone into one box or style. We also need to allow teachers to bring in their own teaching styles. After all, if that soul has chosen a path of teaching, it has inner wisdom and knowledge that can benefit the next generation more than the way the system says it should or the curriculum allows.

It's a good point to make that teachers are not the problem with education. Rather, it's the overall agenda set by those in higher positions. Even teachers have to abide by the rules set by the powers that be, even if they don't agree with them. Teachers do the best they can with the permissions they have. They don't make the curriculum but just teach it to the next generation, not because they want to see us as robots but because they are not aware of the true agenda in place. They just think that they are helping young people with their understanding of the world around them.

It's not the teachers or the schools but those who are pulling the strings, setting the curriculum, and creating the agenda. It's the ones we can't see who are purposely creating this failing system that ultimately benefits the few who are normally are linked or related to those in positions of power. Again, those in power do not want to let go of their hold on humanity, nor do they want the companies that are being used to keep us ill and keep us consuming to be taken over by anyone but those in the bloodline. Why? Because only those in the bloodline are aware of the true agenda regarding these corporations and the cabal in general.

If outsiders were to get in, they might start to change things, and the powers that be don't want that. They fear change, which is why they have created a system in which they have control over the collective beliefs and cause us to fear change. They use our energies against us to create that which they wish to see.

Now that we have a clearer idea of what is going on with the educational system, we can start to make suggestions that benefit the masses, are fair to all, and include all types of learning. Rather than tailoring the student to the school, tailor the school to the student.

What can be done to raise the vibration of the educational system?

First things first, we must not send hate or resentment for the agenda of education but send love and forgiveness, much like the idea of sending love and forgiveness to the governments. It is the same here. We must use our Divine gifts and energy to release the old while holding the vision of the new by using the power of the collective imagination. Only by doing so can we release the resistance and created anew.

Resistance only creates persistence. If we just send hate, resentment, and anger to these situations, we will only increase the power and hold they have over us. Therefore, the first thing we need to do is release the negative energy we hold over those who have created this agenda and send love and forgiveness.

We must take away all the excessive competition and start to balance it with collaboration. Yes, competition is good, but only when it is in balance with its counterpart, collaboration. We must work together rather than against one another.

We need to introduce lessons of spirituality, metaphysics, soul,and universal laws so that people have a good understanding of who they truly are, what they are doing here, and the Divine abilities we all have. This understanding would eliminate the rising numbers of young people who are just confused about who they are, and there purpose here on Earth. This will heal the mental problems and insecurities many have, as well as create space for Divine inventions such as technology which is for the benefit of mother earth and humanity for resolving the issues the world faces. Let's remember that all trouble where spiritually created and thus can only be spiritually resolved.

We need to focus on what needs healing in this world and create that. One way of doing so is to ask our children, "If there were one problem in this world that you could solve, what would it be?" rather than "What do you want to be?" We could also get them to focus on the unique gifts they have to give to the world. By doing so, we would move into soul and spirit, allowing that soul to come forth and show what it is here to do and where its true unique talent lies.

We need to recruit not those who just have qualifications on paper but those who are qualified at a soul level—this is true not only for teachers but all careers. We need to focus on the talents or gifts the individual has come to this plain to share with the world and how best to develop that gift because the gift will benefit us all.

We all have a unique gift that nobody else has. That gift is meant to be harnessed and shared. If we do that, then we can focus on the type of educational plan for that soul, what works for the progression of that soul at different levels, and what best benefits its progression in mind, body, and spirit. We need to allow young people to have a say. We need to allow them to bring forth the wisdom that they have come here to bring rather than tell them what to think and what is right, and wrong/ We need to work together to bring forth a new approach. It is clear that the old paradigm is failing which presents us with the perfect time to bring about a new paradigm.

Rather than focusing on the material world and where we can fit the youth of the modern generation to keep the status quo, we need to focus on how we can incorporate and strengthen every soul's unique talent by looking at what areas on Earth need improvement. We can happily agree that most areas need change and improvement.

We also need to reintroduce lessons in meditation, consciousness and mindfulness, life and its basics, and (a big one for me), emotions. Yes, emotions.

Think back to being a child, can you remember a time when emotions were explained to you? When each emotion and how it manifests was explained? The answer for me is no. I believe that if children were given lessons in these areas, they wouldn't be faced with mental problems, insecurities, and the ever-increasing feeling of being confused and useless. A lot of our children feel confused about their sexuality, feelings, bodies, lives, purpose, and much of the feelings most of the world feels today. It's time to take back our power, our children's power, and our education systems' power and bring forth the new age of teaching—or shall we call it the new/old age of remembering.

We simply need to bring in right-sided brain activity in balance with the left side. That will bring unity and harmony within one's being. (If you need a refresher on right-side and left-side brain functions, jump back to Figure 16.)

Deepak Chopra wrote *The Seven Spiritual Laws of Success*. In that book, he introduced a new idea and belief to his children and the amazing effect of instilling that belief had on his children:

> **I did this with my own children. Again, and again, I told them there was a reason why they were here, and they had to find out what that reason was for themselves. From the age of four years, they *heard* this. I also taught them to meditate when they were about the same age, and I told them, "I never, ever want you to worry about making a living. If you're unable to make a living when you grow up, I'll provide for you, so don't worry about that. I don't want you to focus on doing well in school. I don't want you to focus on getting the best grades or going to the best colleges. What I really want you to focus on is asking yourself how you can serve humanity and asking yourself what your unique talents are. Because you have a unique talent that no one else has, and you have a special way of expressing that talent, and no one else has it." They ended up going to the best schools, getting the best grades, and even in college, they are unique in that they are financially self-sufficient because they are *focused on what they are here to give*.[6]**

It just goes to show that with a change of focus, new perspectives will arise.

---

[6]. Chopra, *The Seven Spiritual Laws of Success*, 96–97.

The Message about Education and the Modern Generation

Education was created so people would participate in politics. Although when education was first introduced it had good intentions, over time those in power that hold control of the direction of education have used education to suit their needs, to keep their companies going, to keep those in power in power.

Although the world has advanced in many areas of the human experience, the school system has not, I must point out this is not being created by headteachers, teachers, but more the those who oversee the education curriculum. Many teachers have left the education sector because they have experienced the true intentions of those who run the education curriculum. If you are interested in learning more, I recommend a book called "the deliberate dumbing down of America" although this is about the American educational system it relates heavily to those in the western world.

We need to remove the age-old format and setup of education and move into the modern world. We need to balance the activities on the right side and left side of the brain and include more lessons on meditation, self-awareness, creativity, and intuition exploration. We need to get rid of extensive computer use and go back to using our physical selves.

We need to allow teachers to bring their wisdom to the children rather than relying on a system that tells them what to teach, what not to teach, and how to teach it. We need to recruit teachers using soul qualifications, not just paper qualifications.

We need to get rid of generic exams and focus on the purpose or the soul, not making more robots to keep the status quo.

Sex and Gender

Everything in the universe has male and female aspects and energies (including me and you), no matter whether it's physically male or female. The idea that we are simply male, or female is a distortion. We all hold equal masculine and feminine aspects and energies within us. We can call this mix the yin and yang of life. We all have the Divine right to express all aspects of the self.

As we have spoken about already, for something to exist, the opposite must also exist. They are not separate but part of the whole experience, just in varying degrees. Therefore, male and female are not opposites but one and the same.

We each hold masculine and feminine energies within our being. They are built into the genetic makeup of all life. But much like all experiences on this plane, the problem we have is that we see everything as physically split—man *or* woman, male *or* female. We need to start seeing the bigger picture, uniting the two gender energies, and bringing understanding of how we hold both energies within us and how focusing on one or other only causes more separation. That is how we can heal the collective karmic gender energy.

Whilst men have been repressed in the expression of the divine feminine energies, women have also been repressed in not only masculine but feminine also. That coupled with the negative perspective of the purpose and role of the divine masculine programmed into women has created a misunderstanding of masculine energy, this misunderstanding has resulted in fear.

To heal this divide, we must see through the separation and acknowledge the repression on both sides. We must take responsibility for what we have caused and created. Only through awareness of our responsibility can we truly heal.

There are a lot of women are feeling the power of the cosmic divine feminine energies we are currently in but are coming from an unconscious space of masculine ego. The ego has tricked women to believe they are coming from a space of divine feminine this unconscious masculine ego control has repressed males also.

They are controlling men's emotions, telling them how to act, look, and think, repressing their sexuality and sexual desires, and leaving men to feel unloved, lonely, unheard, and unexpressed. At the same time, women are angry because they attract men who they feel don't love them or who hurt them or because men are not living up to the expectations they set. Yet men act this way because they don't express their emotions. This is due to the repressing in male's divine feminine energies, this repression is the result of why men often feel confused about how they feel and why they struggle to express emotion to others.

This repression is plain to see. If a man wishes to attract a woman or express his sexual desire, he must jump through the hoops of female expectations. Even if he does that, there is a high chance that the woman will judge and shame the man. A man complimenting a woman or expressing his sexual desire is judged as perverted, yet it is acceptable for a woman to do the same to both men and women. I observe this a lot. You only have to look at social media to see the way women see men. It is not just society that is causing this separation, but many spiritualist groups and so-called gurus are doing it too.

The same thing has happened across history due to the switch back to the collective feminine Earth energy, and it had also been done to women. They have been repressed in not only their natural feminine expressions but also their masculine energies, being told how to think, look, and be, what they can and can't do, and to repress their sexual expression and desires. That is the reason why there is such much deep-seated resentment towards men and t why there is such a lack of understanding on both sides. It's like we are playing a game of revenge—they did it to us, so we will do it to them.

This to-and-fro of patriarchy and matriarchy is the reason for such extensive repression and resentment in both men and women and the creation of such intense karmic energy. This way of thinking will not heal anything. The way we heal these karmic patterns is to understand and take responsibility for equally creating repression in one another for the benefit of the powers that be and the system in place. We must take responsibility and acknowledge the Divine truth: we equally hold masculine and feminine energies within us.

Because of this incorrect thinking and programming, we have tuned out the opposite aspects of our beings, which has created disharmony and imbalance not only between the genders but also within the self. To truly bring balance to the collective and ourselves, we must tune into both aspects of our energy. We must Align the yin and yang aspects and make the circle whole.

The system has stamped out many forms of feminine energy and expression, not only in men but also in women. That is why women have such resentment towards men and why females have such fear of the expression of masculine energy.

Male and females need to collectively embrace and allow both their masculine and feminine energies and expression to come forth and join in unity. Equally, males need to come out of this overly male-dominated energy and allow themselves to express their female aspects, such as emotion, nurturing, and intuition. Both genders need to be allowed to express their sexuality and sexual desire free of judgments and shame.

Let's look at what are the main aspects of males and female expression.

The symbol of Mars (known as a warrior planet) or male can be depicted as ♂, which is the hermetic symbol for Mars, or as □. Typical male energy traits include logic, reason,

rationality, and strength. The symbol of Venus (known as the planet of
 Divine love) or female can be depicted as ♀, the hermetic symbol for Venus, or as ○. Typical female energy traits include intuition, expression, creativity, and emotion

We all have these energy traits and, at one point or another, have expressed these traits. We are equal in Divine feminine and masculine energies.

For eons, the Divine aspects and expression of the Divine feminine have been degraded, mocked, and oppressed not only for women but also for men. This ridicule is the design of those who wish to control the masses to stop the rising of the individual and the collective consciousness. Feminine energy is needed to raise one's consciousness above the ego, get into the heart, connect with the higher self, and bring in remembrance of who one truly is and what one is doing here.

Here on Earth, we are told that to be the definition of male and attractive to females, we must be big, strong, and muscular, have a high social status, do this job and not that, not express emotion and vulnerability, wear this and not that, and act this way and not that way. Equally, women are told that they must be petite and physically weak, have certain aesthetic assets and look a certain way, act like this and not like that, do this job and not that, and wear this and not wear that. All of this is a complete lie created by mainstream media, religion, and the system to keep us all repressed in emotions and expression and to keep the patriarchy and matriarchy revenge going. They have turned us against ourselves not only individually but also collectively, physically, and mentally. They have stopped us from uniting, understanding, and raising our consciousness, ultimately keeping them in their positions of power and creating more profits and control over the masses.

Make no mistake, there is nothing wrong with girls wanting to wear blue instead of pink, play sports, or dig for worms rather than play with dolls. But here in this realm, we judge and label these girls as "tomboys" when it is really just a perfectly natural expression of the soul's Divine masculine. Equally, there is nothing wrong with boys wanting to wear pink or play with dolls, expressing their Divine feminine energies of nurturing and caring. These are natural healthy expressions.

The repression of gender energy is a part of the major mental confusion and emotional repression we see in the world today for both males and females. Instead, let's embrace the opposite energy aspects of our being. Males need to come out of such dominating male energy and start allowing themselves to express their feminine aspects, caring and nurturing themselves and others without judging themselves and others as weak, allowing themselves to express and be gentle on themselves. Females need to start to express their female energies and their masculine aspects, such as logic, reason and strength, without the fear of judgment from others and themselves. They need to release the belief that masculine energy is just aggression and domination. That is how we can create balance and harmony within the mind, body, and spirit and within humanity. We will be able to heal much of the repression of the All. We then start to fully understand ourselves, and when we know and understand ourselves, we can know and understand one another.

We need to release the judgments and blame set upon everything. While those in power have created this imbalance for their own agenda, we can bring it back into harmony through our collective love and Divine understanding. Once we move away from this blame and judgment and start to take reasonability for the energy aspects within each of us, we can bring unity, energy balance, understanding, and healing for the repression of all opposite gender energy expression karma, which will result in pure, non-judgmental love of the soul expression of each gender and the collective. We are told that to be a man or woman, we must be a certain thing or act a certain way. We need to heal and move away from this thinking.

We also need to redefine gender roles. A balance of both energies is necessary to progress, heal, and move humanity and its collective consciousness forward. We need to become aware of and eliminate gendered job stereotyping (labels). We need to eliminate the idea that men can only express certain emotions to seen as "real men" (i.e., that they can't cry or show vulnerability). We need to eliminate the idea that women must repress certain male energy traits to be seen as "real women" and not tomboys. We need to eliminate the idea that only women can be nurses and only men can doctor's or the idea that only women can be midwives and only men mechanics. We must allow each to openly and freely express whatever aspect of the energy he or she wishes to express free of judgment if we want to bring healing to the psyche of humanity.

Another way we need to do this is to redefine gender roles, as a balance of both energies is necessary for humanity and its collective consciousness to progress, heal and move forward.

We need to become aware of and eliminate gender/ job roles stereotyping (labels), this is the idea that men can only express certain emotions to seen as a "real man" i.e. not cry or show vulnerability, and women to repress certain male energy traits to be seen as "a real woman" and not a tomboy, also the idea that only women can be nurses and men doctors, or the idea that only women can be midwives, and men mechanics, we must allow each to openly and freely expresses whatever aspect of the energy they wish free of judgement if we wish to bring healing to the psyche of humanity.

The system knows the damage this stereotyping is causing and is using it to its advantage.

When watching TV, have you ever noticed how adverts to do with children and care always have women with little to no men, but ads for the DIY and car-related things only show men? This is yet another way the system uses the media to force public opinion and push the stereotyping we see in the world today. It uses subliminal messaging and repetition to subconsciously implant the idea that certain emotional roles and jobs are meant for one gender and not the other, creating frustration, disharmony, and imbalance within the consciousness of humanity. We are all here to express, play, and be whatever we want, including the jobs we have, our gender expression, and our full emotional range.

The stress on the genders to be as we tell them to be, to feel how we tell them they can feel, only creates insecurities and resentment, leading to a greater lack of self-love for all. The expectations we place on each other cause the mental and emotional problems much of humanity faces.

Insecurities in men are things such as not being able to support their families, not being finically stable, and not being physically strong enough to protect their woman. After all, society says these things create "real" men or that they're a "man's" job, which is simply not true. This messaging puts pressure on men of the world to live up to the expectations of society.

Similarly, women are told that they should be housewives, should cook and clean, and should keep the children in check. Again, this messaging creates pressure on those who want to do more, such as women who want to focus on a career rather than looking after the children and those who feel they don't live up to the gender expectations of society. Perhaps one is struggling with being a parent, which is nothing to be ashamed of or depressed about. Raising a child is one of the hardest things to do. But these expectations have been created as a way to create mental and emotional repression within the minds of humanity for both genders.

We need to release our judgments of one another and allow everyone to express themselves and bring masculine and feminine energy into and balance, re-connect with the right-sided brain functions, rebalance ourselves, and get back in touch with our intuition, emotions, and expressions.

The below statements outline the divine feminine and divine masculine ideals, which bring perfect harmony with both aspects.

A healthy representation of the Divine Masculine is witnessed through a person who is strong, but gentle. He has an appropriate action of guidance and leadership without the need of praise or ego-stroking. He turns away from greed and conflict and instead stays in a space of honor, honesty, and diplomacy. He is confident but not arrogant, and adventurous but not reckless. He is someone you want to follow and makes you feel safe, supported and protected either physically, emotionally, or spiritually.

A healthy representation of the Divine Feminine is kind, generous, wise and supportive. With the continued growth of mankind dependent on the health of its women, the Divine Feminine represents the ultimate mother–fertile, intuitive, patient, nurturing and healing. She is the representation of growth, not just in a physical way, but also emotionally and spiritually. We all birth something – an idea, a friendship, a business plan, a family – and it is the Divine Feminine within us all that brings it into full fruition.[7]

It will be perfectly fine, and all will benefit all if we allow ourselves to express our gender energy opposites. Doing so will bring any overexpressed energy traits into balance. I often say that which we repress early in life will only get exacerbated later in life or cause resentment. Only through pure non-judgmental expression can love be seen and felt. When we do

---

7. "Divine Balance, When Masculine Aligns with Feminine," Beyond the Ordinary Show, https://www.beyondtheordinaryshow.com/spiritual-dictionary/divine-balance-masculine-feminine/.

so, those overly expressive tendencies will harmonize and bring harmony to us and healing to all.

What about transgender and homosexuality? Both have been around since time began. They are not anything new. There have even been depictions of such experiences as far back as ancient Egypt.

There is nothing wrong with being homosexual or transgender. The soul might want to experience both genders in one lifetime to gain a deeper understanding of the physical and energetic differences or simply to understand its own gender on a deeper level. That may be a reason why a soul would choose an experience of homosexuality, but ultimately, only the soul itself will know (consciously or unconsciously) the reason for choosing that experience.

The problem we have is not the acceptance of these gender types but the agenda to confuse and manipulate young, innocent, vulnerable minds by pushing these ideas into the subconscious and creating even more gender confusion, often at a very early age when the child is still developing his or her self-understanding. This agenda is by design. It causes more confusion and repression, thus making it easier for the system to manipulate and control us, eliminate procreation, and take away the right to raise our children so that the government can do it instead and create more slaves and soldiers of the system.

A few months back, I saw how the education system is going to start to introduce transgender history and have adults go to schools and talk to three- to five-year-old about gender and what it means to be transgender. This program is not to bring awareness to the children but to create subconscious emotional confusion. All children at that age want to do is be children, not think about how they feel or what they want to be. This program is a part of the attempt to create mind control and stop reproduction.

We are at level critical regarding resources and population. When a child goes down the transgender route, he or she becomes a child of the state. The government takes control away from the parents and becomes the parent, making it easier to manipulate the younger generation and creates more profits. We are all aware that the cosmetic industry creates billions through mental manipulation and public opinion.

I'm not saying there aren't children who feel that they're in the wrong body, because their souls genuinely feel they are. But due to the lack of understanding of the soul, we have forgotten about past lives and other soul factors. A lot of the time, these feelings are derived from the energy of past lives or past karma and often are overcome through soul understanding and not cosmetic alterations.

We need to stop creating these beliefs in children. It's not the children themselves but us who are creating the idea and belief. We just need to allow the children to be children. Let them make their own choices. In time, if a child feels this way about him- or herself, he or she will make it known. But the point is that the system doesn't want your children to think for themselves, to make their own choices. The state wants them to be consumer robots and will do and say anything to reach this goal. Ask yourself is this agenda IS really to bring awareness or to bring confusion.

As I mentioned earlier in this book, we all have multiple lives and some reoccurring lives (the same human experience as you may be having now). It is during these lives when a soul can create karmic energy and bring forth the feeling of being in the wrong body. It is very possible that a child was the opposite sex in a past life, and that could be the reason why the child feels that he or she is in the wrong body. With the right understanding, these experiences can be healed through past-life regression and karmic healing, without the need to pay for cosmetics.

Kids and toddlers are curious souls newly in the body. They want to explore, feel, and experience everything, and they do so without self-judgment. That includes boys wanting to play with dolls and girls wanting to play with cars. It is just their expression of their masculine and feminine energies, which is perfectly natural. It is humanity (adults) who has created labels and lower vibrations for opposite gender expression, which then become the children's beliefs.

These misguided beliefs can create two things:

- gender confusion, which ends up becoming insecurities and anxieties.
- a continuous cycle of misunderstanding and judgment, forming insecurities and anxieties due to a lack of compassion or understanding that are passed on to their children and so on.

To stop this cycle, we need to change our thoughts and perspective. That is how we create anew. Remember, it's all about the thought, which gives the perspective, which in turn gives you your perception.

The government has put in place a medical scheme in which toddlers who feel confused about their gender are raised by the government rather than their parents, but people over the age of twelve must undergo intensive physiological assessment for two years. Young, innocent minds are more impressionable than the minds of people entering their teens. They say that children's minds are most susceptible to the influences of the external world up to the age of seven, and they are especially susceptible to false core belief programming. After that, the mind becomes stubborn. Awareness and soul understanding of this fact is the first stage in changing how we perceive these experiences.

Now, let's talk about sex and sexuality, one of the biggest taboos of life. Why? Because of organized religion and the social elite's agenda uses it against us without us knowing to lower its natural vibration (sound familiar?) and because we have continued to create and build this belief within ourselves and our children. We now have so much sexual dysfunction, inhibition, and violence within humanity because of this repression.

As I have previously mentioned, there are no sins and no commandments about who and what you should be. You are not being judged and will not be judged for what you think or do. It is no different when it comes to sex.

So much distortion has been placed around this act and expression we call sex that we have got to the point where its deemed "wrong" to do, "bad" to talk about, and "perverted" to experiment with. However, the Divine truth is it is fine to have as much sex as you want. You are encouraged to play and experiment with it, your genitals, and your creative energy. The Great Spirit does not and will not judge you nor discourage you from enjoying your body or having or playing with sex. After all, sex is a wholly (holy) natural human expression and built within the biological makeup of humans.

That being said, it is wise to understand that over-indulgence in sexual activity can be very unhealthy and dampen our power of mental self-control. I will discuss this a later on.

The distortion of sex and sexuality was purposeful. It is a way to control the masses and create separation between one another and ourselves, creating more fear-based beliefs about ourselves, our purpose, and our essence, leading to the repression of sexual expression and the love of we truly are. Sex is the most beautiful expression of this truth of who we are, and our repression has caused so much guilt, shame, inhibition, and overall sexual dysfunction that we unhealthily hold in our minds and bodies.

If there were no sexual repression, there would be no rape or sexual abuse. As with all repressed human emotions, these acts are derived from extreme emotional repression—in this case, sexual repression. Whenever we repress an emotional aspect of the human experience, we cause it to be exacerbated later on in life. Anything caged will always attempt to break free and be angry that it has been kept from feeling freedom.

The glamour and porn industry were also born from this repression. Porn is just the collective expression of repressed sexuality. It is simply souls expressing their inner desires, showing that their sexuality cannot and will not be repressed.

The main issue here is what organized religion and the system have done with sex and sexuality and caused us to believe and create for ourselves and our children. Just like it has done with all Divine gifts and messages, it has lowered the vibration of sexual energy and action and is now using it against us to create insecurities, fear, separation, and domination. This view causes us to come from the root chakra rather than feeling and having sex from the whole body.

Sex is a perfectly natural human expression and is the most powerful physical expression of love. It is not wrong nor bad to have it or to want it. After all, it creates life, and it feels so good. What a blessing it is that the Great Spirit gave us this expression to discover more about who we truly are and who we wish to be.

Sex should not be used to dominate others. Unfortunately, some people use it for this purpose. We often see that in the modern porn industry. The system has corrupted that form of repressed expression and used it against us, which is why sexual domination is pushed on to us through music and media. This idea of using sex to dominate is why many do not feel the true power of sex and the wholeness of expression and often feel unsatisfied.

Sex is simply a pure, loving energy exchange (synergy energy exchange or soul energy exchange). It is just another expression of love in a physical form. It was meant for us to express and experience the feeling of oneness and energies merging. It is a way to not only create life but also experience life. It is an energy we can utilize not only physically but also mentally.

A lot of people—especially those in the spiritual community—believe that to be "enlightened" or "spiritual," you must give up all sexual acts and become abstinent. As good as that might sound, it will not cause more soul or spiritual growth than participating in sexual acts. In fact, abstaining from sex can slow down the process of gaining a true understanding of spirituality, the soul, and its expression. Sex, sexuality, and spirituality go hand in hand. By repressing your sexual expression, you are repressing a part of the whole you. You will never be whole by dismissing sex and sexuality in your human experience.

The idea that one must give up all sexual acts because they're lower vibration acts is yet another distortion created by organized religion and the system to separate us and move us away from oneness, prevent self-love, stop the enjoyment of the body, create insecurities, create judgments, and stop people from reproducing. Plus, as I have already mentioned, when we are in a low vibrational state, we are easier to control and manipulate.

When it comes to sex, most people in the world hold a collective belief that we can only have sex for the purposes of procreation. When we use sex to play or as a means of innocent playfulness we are judged and labelled. Due to the programming of organized religion we hold the belief firmly in the subconscious that God only wants us to have and experience sexual relations with only one person in a lifetime and only for the purpose of procreation and expressing love for that one person, Because of this programming people believe that sex can only be used in that way and not for joy nor pleasure. It most certainly cannot be used in such a way which prevents conception, and although sex is divine, it cannot be used for the means of pleasure without possibility of procreation. This widespread belief has been formed to purposely create fear of God, which in turn creates fear of expressing divine love. Holding this belief has caused humanity to think that sex without possibility of procreation is unnatural, shameful and against the will of the Great Spirit.

These two ideas of sex being both pleasurable and shameful in this construction has created emotional manipulation and confusion. On one hand it has created excitement, wonder, joy and passion, but on the other it has created guilt, fear and shame around sexual desires, fantasies and experiences.

It is a common misconception that sexual energy and spiritual energy do not mix. The idea that people cannot be spiritual if they are sexual is an age-old belief derived from organized religion. We have been told that sexual energy is a "lower chakra" energy and that each energy opposes one another, so if spiritual people wish to seek spiritual growth, they must not engage in any sexual acts and, in many cases, must remain abstinent. We hold this idea as a belief because its "what God wants." But that's not true/ The Great Spirit wants only what we want, and by enjoying sex, we raise our vibrations from lower energies to higher energies.

It is a widely held belief that sex in particular ways, even if it is between a husband and wife is "wrong" or "unnatural" and, therefore, immoral. This belief is derived from those who wrote such commandments, saying, "God wants sexual experiences to occur in a particular way, and if it is not done that way, then you will be sent to hell." You know that place that doesn't exist other than in the illusions of fear. The fear of hell is one of the biggest ways those who control us implemented this belief. They use the fear of God, and all will obey.

We hold a lot of our core beliefs because of the idea of hell and because we have been told it is what God wants when the Great Spirit only wants what we want. After all, it is experiencing itself as us and through us.

We not only find it embarrassing to talk about sex with family and friends but have also been taught not to talk about it in public because it is "wrong," resulting in more repression of sexuality and further separation from our true expressions and oneness of expression. In most cultures, we don't even refer to our sexual body parts by their proper name. The words "penis" and "vagina" are not to be used in public unless it is for medical reasons. But even then, never with small children around. Instead, we use words like "pee-pee" and "lady flower." This terminology has created false beliefs of shame and guilt within humanity's consciousness, subconsciously agreeing that those body parts are not to be named but something to hide, to be embarrassed by, or shameful about. And it starts from the moment you are born.

Consider this: how do we expect our offspring to be confident and at peace in their physical bodies if we teach them to cover up and be ashamed at any given moment? Think back to being a child and your mother or father telling you to put clothes on or to stop playing with your penis or vagina with little to no explanation. Those moments instill these core beliefs of body shame and embarrassment without anyone noticing that they are doing that. Of course, your mother or father was not telling you to cover up so that you would form these beliefs, they were simply passing down what had been told to them from their external influences—parents, grandparents, teachers, religious leaders—who were only passing on what they had been taught and experienced. And so, the cycle continues.

Even as we get older, we are told not to have sex or express our sexuality. We have created labels and judgments as a way to stop us expressing this experience: slag, slut, whore, ho, man-slut, player—the list of repression goes on.

If people cannot speak the names of their body parts, then it creates the belief that people must not show them. I mean, if we can't speak the words, how can we ever be comfortable expressing these parts? We just can't. Only when we redefine sex and its expression can we move forward and heal the mental issues we have regarding sex—the action and expression and its purpose.

Much of humanity feels that certain body parts should and must be covered up because they are deemed too arousing, too shameful, or in many instances, both. In certain places, it is even illegal with punishment in civil law for those who don't obey these rules. This belief and repression have made it so that we see the naked body as something sexual and not just perfectly natural. We have been taught to hide ourselves and our bodies and only display it in acts of sexual expression. Therefore, the human body is now seen as an object rather than an expression of the beauty of the soul.

While the misunderstanding of the body as an object is true for everyone, it is mainly aimed at women (although, today, it happens with men, too). Through this belief and the creations of the porn industry and the modeling industry, which were created from our own collective repressed sexual expression, humans very rarely look past the psychical aesthetics of a person. We determine one's beauty based on the body alone. We are all human. We all like what we like physically, whether it's a certain weight, eye color, breast size, ass, face, chest, height, ab definition, or genitals. There is nothing wrong with that. The problem is when we focus on nothing but the physical, forgetting the beauty of the whole being and soul.

Our repression doesn't stop there. Humanity perceive images depicting sexual expressions in pictures, photos, magazines, video games, tv and movies are distasteful, disgusting and wrong, whilst graphic depictions of murder, war and violence are completely accepted and promoted. Also whilst mainstream media tells us to be ashamed of and embarrassed by our naked bodies, it also creates the propaganda to again form public opinion around what is deemed acceptable, this propaganda has and continues to form mass insecurities within the consciousness of men and women, again using outlets such as TV, books, magazines, radio, film and the internet.

Just because one is physically beautiful, that doesn't mean that person is expressing that level of beauty in his or her intentions and interactions with daily life. Mainstream knows this and wants to keep you in that mindset. That is why the global elites have created the idea and public opinion (through media) that women should be petite, slim, and toned with big breasts and big asses to be sexy or desirable. It is why they have created the idea that men should be tall, muscular, and have huge penises to be attractive. The powers that be know that we are all different, including out body types, structures, and assets. They use this fact against us by creating insecurities in those who don't have socially acceptable bodies, which lowers their vibrations and creates mental illness and physical diseases. It also encourages us hand over our Divine power and be told what is sexy and acceptable, creating money for the cosmetic industry, which fuels the medical, modeling, and porn industries.

There is nothing wrong with modeling, be it topless or high fashion, nor with being a porn star (the soul chooses what the soul chooses). And again, let's remind ourselves that porn and modeling are just collective creations of repressed sex and sexual expression. Regardless of how we judge it, it's all just experiences for the soul. But the problem with these creations is the agenda to create negative core beliefs and insecurities within the consciousness about sex, sexuality, self-image, and self-worth. These industries focus on the physical, suggesting what is good sex, what is a big penis and what is small, what a nice set of breasts looks like, what a good derriere looks like, how women should act sexually, how men should act sexually, and what is a good amount of time to have sex. These industries are instilling negative core programming and mass insecurities about the act of sex, the body, and true intimacy.

Although there is nothing wrong or bad with porn or modeling (because there is no such thing as good or bad), the truth is the agenda and intention are not positive. Although these industries were created as forms of sexual expression because of our collective repression, the powers that be have infiltrated them and distorted their original purpose. These industries now not only create insecurities in the minds of humanity but also promote sex to control and dominate. It is just another way to lower the vibration of our Divine bodies and the expression of sexuality.

It is well known that even people within these industries are harshly judged. Some are told to increase their breast size, to workout, or have cosmetic surgery. It said that most porn stars and models last three months before leaving. There are many accounts from ex-porn stars and models who openly divulge the agenda of certain companies.

As much as I say that porn is not wrong, as nothing is "bad" in the realm of the third dimension, it must be brought to the consciousness that porn is creating the negative beliefs that we must be aggressive, controlling, and dominating in sex. It is plain to see with the major rise in extreme bondage, BDSM, and anal penetration not only within the porn industry but within all media outlets, music and film being major contributors. This agenda and the fact that humanity says you can't be spiritual and sexual is creating the psychological and physical problems we see in our human experience regarding our bodies and mental attitudes towards sex. That is not to say that we can't experiment by trying a little bondage, anal, or dominance, but it has to be done with pure positive intentions and consent.

Now we have a clearer picture of the reasons for our sexual repression, we can start using our awareness to shed light on the understanding and experience of gender and sex. First, we need to apply this new perspective and understanding to our spirits, unifying sexuality and spirituality under one understanding from a place of Divine love. We need to embrace sex and its full expression, understanding that sexual unions are amazing and wonderful expressions of the oneness we are. They are extraordinarily powerful and deeply meaningful experiences of the most intimate physical, emotional, psychological, and spiritual aspects of the self that people can share with one another. They are celebrations of love, oneness, and life.

We also need to be aware that sexual energy is a powerful mental tool that we can use to manifest our dreams and visions. That is what is meant by raising our sexual energy through to the higher chakras. It doesn't mean not to have sex nor enjoy it. When we speak of raising sexual energy, we are simply moving away from the thought that we must use sex as a way to control, dominate, and manipulate and that we must be like this and perform like that and toward a thought and feeling of the love of the pure expression, the love of joining in oneness, and the love of exploring one another's bodies and sexual desires without domination, manipulation, and control. It is also an understanding that the term also refers to using sexual energy mentally, not just physically. This perspective is raised sexual energy—feeling and have sex from the whole body, not just the lower chakra energy of lust alone while recognizing the creative power of expressed sexual energy.

We need to remove all taboos about sex from both children and adults and see that sex is a beautifully natural act meant to be experienced by consenting souls in whatever way brings pleasure and respects the boundaries, desires, and agreements of all involved. We need to see the body for what it is: a sacred vessel with nothing to be ashamed of or embarrassed by, understanding that no part of the body is anything but beautifully divine and, therefore, may be shown and seen without shame and judgment through the eyes of the Great Spirit. Again, this is an expression of higher chakra sexual energy.

Regardless of what we find attractive or sexy, we must accept that we all see through different eyes, and what is sexy or attractive to one person may not be to another. What we call sexy or beautiful differs for everyone, and we should accept people without labels and judgment.

When we start to see from this perspective, magical things can happen. Sexual guilt and sexual shame will virtually disappear from the human experience, and so will sexual assault. We may see sexual expression being lifted to the level of the Divine (joy, playfulness, love, pleasure, harmony, oneness, and compassion) and never lowered to the level of the ego (need, control, manipulation, and dominance). There will be no thought that spiritual energy and sexual energy do not mix, but rather, it will be taught that sexual energy is a beautiful expression of spiritual energy in a physical form that comes from the whole body, not this age-old belief of just lower energy expression. They are, in fact, of the same energies.

As I have already stated, there is nothing wrong with sexual expression, but overindulgence in sexual activity is also not healthy for the body or soul. Sexual energy is so powerful that if it is not controlled, it can be very addictive. As with any addiction, it is not healthy for the mind, body, or soul because the mind will be dominated by thoughts of sexual desire, leaving no room for anything else.

When we feel sexual energy, we spend most of our time trying to find ways to fulfill the urge, which takes away our concentration, the power of a balanced mind, and the power of being in the moment. Eventually, this urge becomes an obsession, which turns into a need, and that need takes away the playfulness of sexual acts and experiences.

Just think back to a time when you were at work, and you suddenly saw someone who you found attractive and aroused you. Your mind probably went completely off the task at hand and straight to your genitals, deep in thoughts of sexual activity with that person. Just imagine how much time is spent on these types of thoughts when faced with these experiences. A lot, right? Now think how much time you could have spent using that same energy and power to complete the task at hand or create something you wish to manifest.

You see, sexual energy is not only powerful in physical acts but is also when combined with creative thought. Combining sexual energy with creative thought or imagination can help manifest the desired results quicker. Because of the very nature of sexual energy as a creative life force, when it is not used in this way, it can create blockages in the lower energy centers, giving us feelings of discontent and dissatisfaction. It is only when we use sexual energy for mental creation and not just for physical pleasure that we feel and gain the real benefits of sexual energy and its whole expression. And in doing so, we attract more wholesome sexual experiences, meaning experiences that are not about pure lust, domination, control, self-gratification, and manipulation.

While it's perfectly fine to have sex, enjoy it, and play with it, it is important to balance and use this energy mentally, and not just for physical acts, which you will find ultimately brings dissatisfaction. Overuse of physical sexual energy will just cause eventual dissatisfaction with physical pleasure; that is why they say sex is a sin. As I mentioned earlier, there are no sins. Acts are labeled sins only because they eventually cause harm through excessive use, not only in the physical sense but in the mental sense, too.

The problem here is that while we are constantly lusting over the activity of sex, we are abusing the power of sexual energy. By "abusing," I mean we are fixating on satisfying sexual urges, having sex because of a feeling of need instead of playfulness. Sexual energy is not meant for physical expression only but also creative mental expression. It's meant to be used and can be used to bring more passion to the business you are working on creating, create the life you desire to experience, and manifest your vision of the future. Longing and lusting for constant sexual activity takes away this mental power.

If we harnessed our sexual power in a more balanced way in mind and body, then we would not feel the need to constantly have sex with people we don't resonate with and don't connect with just to satisfy the urge. We would be more balanced, more successful, and happier with the sex we are having and the life we are experiencing. W would also stop absorbing the negative energies others carry with them. Remember, sex is an energy transfer, so when we have sex with someone who we don't feel a connection with, we are absorbing energies we may not want in our aura. In many cases, it also creates attachments to people who we don't want in our experience.

Once we have healed and understood sex and sexuality in its soul entirety, using it not just for physical expression but also for mental creativity expression, then we have moved the energy up through the chakras from the lower chakra to not only the higher but all chakras.

How do we use sexual energy mentally? When we think of sexual energy, we immediately think of intercourse, but what we have forgotten is we can access and use this same energy to bring more creative force to our visions and more passion and motivation to our tasks at hand or life goals. By focusing on the root chakra and our thoughts, we can bring this energy up into the sacral chakra, which is where great ideas can be inspired.

Sexual energy is known as kundalini energy. It is the sexual energy stored at the base of the spine at the root. Once this energy is raised, it not only brings higher sexual pleasure but can also heal, inspire, motivate, and creative.

To summarize, sex is perfectly fine to have, and enjoy, and play with as much as you want with whomever you want so long as it's with consent on both sides, coming from an energy of playfulness rather than need, and not used to dominate, control, manipulate, or bring self-gratification. But remember that sexual energy is also the driving force of creative energy, and while physical acts of sex are great and will not be judged, overindulgence will lower your brain power, concentration, and mind power and will eventually make sex dissatisfying. That said, when you do bring into balance the understanding of sexual energy, you will create better sexual experiences and a deeper love of the self and one another.

Deepak Chopra has written a few books about this subject. Here is a sample from his book *Kama Sutra & The Seven Spiritual Laws of Love*. In a blog post about this book, he wrote about the twelve laws of sexual energy, and I must say they fit right into what I have mentioned above.

1. **Sexual energy is the primal and creative energy of the universe. All things that are alive come from sexual energy. In animals and other life forms, sexual energy expresses itself as biological creativity. In humans, sexual energy can be creative at all levels – physical, emotional and spiritual. In any situation, where we feel attraction, arousal, awakening, alertness, passion, interest, inspiration, excitement, creativity, enthusiasm, in each of these situations, sexual energy is at work. Whenever we feel these states of awareness, we must put our attention on the energy that we are experiencing, nourishing it with our attention, experiencing it with joy and keeping it alive in our awareness.**

2. **Sexual desire is sacred and chaste. The suppression of sexual energy is false, ugly and unchaste.**

3. **During sexual union, there is union between flesh and spirit.**

4. **Bliss, carefreeness and playfulness are the essence of sex.**

5. To improve your sexual experiences, get rid of your expectations. Expectations are primarily in three areas: 1) Performance, exemplified in the question, "How am I doing?" 2) Feeling, exemplified in the question, "How am I feeling?" 3) Security, exemplified in the question, "Do you love me?"

6. In sex, as in all areas of life, resistance is born of fear. All resistance is mental. It implies judgment against what is being felt. Sex becomes a problem when it gets mixed with hidden emotions such as shame, guilt and anger.

7. Sexual intimacy is the road to the taste or experience of true freedom, because it is the one area of life in which we can become completely uninhibited and free.

8. Sexual fulfillment occurs when the experience comes from playfulness instead of need. Frequently people bring their conflicts and needs into the sexual experience. When sex is used to fulfill needs, it leads to addiction. When sex comes from playfulness, the result is ecstasy.

9. All problems related to sex, neurosis, deviancy, sexual misbehavior, violence, abuse, can be traced to resistance, to suppression and repression, not to the sexual urges themselves. If we are allowed to discover our urges, desires and emotions, without outside inhibition, they won't go to extremes. Extremism, in any form, is a reaction to repression, inhibition and suppression.

Aggression and violence are the shadow energies of fear and impotence.

10. Sex is a means of escaping our little self or ego. It is many peoples' only experience of meditation.

11. Meaningful sex has to be value based. Values are personal. Each situation that has sexual energy in it, involves the whole human being and their entire value system. My values may be different from yours, and I have no right to be the moral judge of anyone's values. It is important, however, to have core values, and respect them. Without values, we become spiritually bankrupt. Sexual experience will never cause problems and will always be joyful, if lovers share the same values.

12. True intimacy is union between flesh and flesh, between subtle body and subtle body, between soul and soul. Sexual energy is sacred energy. When we

13. have restored the sexual experience to the realm of the sacred, our world will be chaste and divine, holy and healed.[8]

The Message about Sex and Gender

Everyone has male and female, whether they are a man or a woman. We all need to allow everyone to express opposite gender tendencies without judging or labeling. When we do so, we will bring balance to the mental gender of humanity.

---

[8]. Deepak Chopra, "Insights into Sex and Spirituality," *The Blog*, *Huffpost*, December 6, 2017, https://www.huffpost.com/entry/kama-sutra-insights-into_b_623177.

Using sex to control, manipulate, and dominate only creates more energy blockages within the body.

Lust is not wrong because it is a healthy part of sexual desire, but you must understand that lust alone gives you only 10% of the beauty of sex, sexuality, and sexual expression and will only serve and satisfy you for so long. Prolonged lusting for sex will result in addiction, which will create negative experiences and energy blockages in the body.

There's nothing wrong with sex and sexual activities if they come from an energy of playfulness and not of need. Overindulgence in sexual activity coming from thoughts and energy of need instead of playfulness will bring addiction and dissatisfaction and stunt your mental power. All addictions come from the need of something rather than the joy of having or experiencing that thing.

Sexual energy is not only for physical acts but to be used and combined with mental creativity by raising the kundalini energy. When used in physical acts of sexual activity, the kundalini energy brings more satisfying and intense orgasms.

Sexual energy not only brings pleasure and joy but can also heal, create, motivate, and inspire.

Each gender can be, do, and express whatever it wishes, regardless of how we perceive "real" men and "real" women. Crying is not just for women, and logic is not just for men.

Global Consciousness

"We are all a perfect idea in the mind of God that is constantly changing. We are all God in the event of experience." —Lee McKeown

As I've mentioned briefly throughout this book, we are creating and healing not only in our individual human experience but we together with all of humanity and the Universe. We are not just co-creating with the Great Spirit for ourselves, but we are creating together the world we perceive. As we head towards the golden age, things are changing because the collective mind is changing. The collective mind is responsible for the world we have experienced. This collective oneness from which we are created has not only created a lower vibrational experience but also healing and balance.

For the world to flow and sustain itself, it has to have a system in which everything has a purpose, a bigger purpose that contributes to everything. The ecosystem, for instance, is a system in which each animal works with another to keep the system thriving. If it weren't for this system of ebb and flow, the animals and us would die out.

We, as humans, are putting the ecosystem out of balance.

We are overfishing, over-killing, and over-consuming. It's no secret that many animals that were once in abundance have become extinct. This result is a pure example of the misbalance in the world we, the collective, have created.

I am not trying to be hard on humanity but simply bring awareness. Anything that has been created and experienced on Earth has been created by the collective. Yes, that includes negativity and low vibrations. True, we didn't ask for war, poverty, an imbalance in resources, the Babylonian system, or to be controlled. We just never did anything about it. We never took any responsibility for ourselves and our collective creation.

There are close to 9 billion souls on Earth today, and less than 1% of the 9 billion own and control the world's wealth and resources and, more to the point, has been allowed too. It is not because they have more power but because we have given them ours. If we hadn't given them our power, they wouldn't have any.

Humanity has handed over its power many times out of fear. It has handed the collective responsibilities over to a lower source, and it has allowed the collective consciousness to be manipulated and controlled to create the world the global elites wish to see, not the world the collective wishes to see. But the global elites tell us all the things you want to hear on TV, on the radio, and in magazines. They have created through us this experience of not wanting responsibility for ourselves, leading us not to want responsibility for ourselves, which has led us to give responsibility for ourselves over to those who don't care about the health and well-being of us or the collective. That is why there is so much misbalance in the world and why the collective has been diseased of late. When I say "diseased," I mean as in "dis-ease." The collective has been out of ease with its Divine alignment.

I have mentioned throughout this book the impact on not just the individual consciousness but the collective consciousness. That impact is that which we perceive on a global scale. We need to heal if the world is to heal, and we need to forgive and release. When we do so, we release and clear space for the new higher-balanced energies, which will heal the world's issues, such as global warming, poverty, war, famine, and all those like energies.

When we heal the collective conscious mind and raise into alignment with the Great Spirit, we will not only create heaven in our personal experiences but also create heaven on Earth for the collective. After all, we are one. We are all souls on a mission to remember who we are through multiple lifetimes and experiences, which bring us closer to the Great Spirit and, as religion puts it, "home to God." But always remember that you must heal yourself and understand the creative power of your own individual consciousness before you can help understand and heal the consciousness of the world.

By taking the suggested actions in this book and researching for yourself who you truly are and what your truth is, we will all contribute to the raising of the collective consciousness. We will allow space for new and old minds to bring forth the technologies that align with the good of Earth and of the people. We will allow the global collective to release old paradigms of fear and judgment, leading to higher mental and soul states that embody collective peace, understanding, and unity. We will inspire and create new innovative ideas to bring the world and its people back into alignment, bringing forth a new system that is free of the low-vibration consciousness, enslavement, separation, and the misbalance we see in the world today.

When we see and visualize everything in harmony, peace, prosperity, and abundance, we will create it.

The Message about Global Consciousness

We are all collectively creating the experience we see on Earth. As we heal ourselves, we begin to heal the world. We are all heading towards remembering the same thing, and that is that we are Divine love.

We can only heal the collective by healing the individual. Collective energy is powerful and creates global changes instantly.

Collectively, we are all reflections of one another, what we need to heal, what we don't want to face, and the love that we each hold, whilst also reflecting the love we are, the potential we each hold within us, if we but re-connect with that forgotten part of ourselves.

Heaven and Hell

This chapter is a short one on the meaning of heaven and hell from the soul perspective. Simply put, heaven and hell are your conscious states of perception in relation to who you think you are or should be.

As I've already mentioned, there is no literal heaven or hell in the way we have been taught. You are not being judged, and you are not going to burn in the pits of hell for your so-called sin or crimes. This concept was developed to simply create fear and a false belief that if you follow the "commandments" that the powers that be and organized religion placed on us, then you will get into heaven, but only if you do as they tell you to do. These rules normally include you being less than that which you truly are (making you less holy than the priest) and require you to pay. organized religion states you can pay to get into heaven. That is a lie to create more profits, control, and fear.

Think of this: The Great Spirit is everything and nothing. It is the air, the water, me, and you; it is all the gold, silver, and diamonds. Now, with this in mind, ask yourself why the Great Spirit would want you to pay it. After all, it is everything, and it has everything and wants for nothing. It is energy. It cares not for the material world—after all, the material world is an illusion (as we have spoken about ready). Everything is energy, even that which we perceive as physical. This idea that you can pay to get into heaven in a lie. No amount of material possessions will get you into heaven. Not only that, but there is no heaven to get into, only that which you wish to create as your personal experience of heaven. Yes, even after the passing from Earth, we are still creating through belief and faith. Creation never stops. After all, it is what we all are.

The whole idea of hell and the devil has become so powerful because the powers that be know that if they instill this fear within us, we will do as we are told. All this belief does is keep us in fear of so-called dying, even though there is no death. Fear of dying stops us from truly living, stops us from living in joy, peace, and happiness, and keeps us in worry, fear, and judgment. That is the whole reason behind the creation of the traditional idea of heaven and hell.

In reality, heaven and hell are the labels for how you not only perceive the world but also use your creative powers in relation to who you are, and their manifestations vary from soul to soul. Essentially, hell to a soul would be living opposite to what it is. That is why Earth has been called hell many times—because much of the population is living in opposite to their true nature. *We* are living in opposite to our true nature. For example, if you are a soul of love (which we all are), living in fear would seem like hell.

The traditional idea of hell and what we have been manipulated to believe is the reason so many souls are self-destructive, thinking, "Well, if I'm going to hell, what's the point? If I'm going to be tortured for eternity, I might as well just sod it all and put myself there." And that is what we do.

Due to the distortion of the message, we have created our own idea of hell and decided to accept it as life and our truth. But it is a lie. The only hell a soul will experience will be its own ego hell that it creates through fear because it is opposite to what it truly is, and that is love!

Where love exists, hell cannot. It's the same as when you think happy thoughts, and negative ones don't exist.

Loneliness can also be perceived as hell. Why? Because it is t opposite to the soul's truth, and that is that we are never alone. Whether we have a family of blood or not, friends, angels, guides, dragons, and many more beings of light wish to guide, help, and support us. It's just that we are either unaware of these beings or energies, or we simply don't believe in them. Remember, believing is seeing! What we believe and think about ourselves, we will experience in our reality. This truth goes back to the whole idea of like attracting like: fear attracts fear, and love attracts love.

Release this fear of the false illusion of hell, and you will start to live life. It's only when we aren't afraid of dying that we can truly start living.

The Message about Heaven and Hell

Hell is a state of mind, not a place. The idea of hell as a place was created to control the masses.

You cannot buy your way into heaven because it is your natural essence. Heaven is simply living in line with your Divine truth: love. You don't have to wait to go to heaven. You can bring heaven to your Earth experience.

Hell isn't real, but if you believe in it heavily, you can create the experience for yourself in both the physical and non-physical.

I Am

Throughout this book, I have continually mentioned how our thoughts and words create our realities. I have done so purposely because it is a message from the soul that we need to take on board and remember if we are going to raise our vibrations and change the lives we are currently experiencing or the perspective from which we are seeing.

The words "I am" have been said throughout history to make powerful statements. Now, all words are powerful, but these words are like a genie in a bottle because with enough emotional energy, whatever follows those words gets created in the physical. That is how the law of attraction works and what Jesus, Abraham, and many others before spoke of.

When we use the words "I am," with its corresponding feeling whether it's positive or negative we are creating an image and making a statement to the Universe through frequency. We are showing the universe through the imagination and feeling what we believe we are and want we want, and because the Universe just sends back what we put out, it reflects exactly what we think we are and want back at us.

When it comes to making wishes to the universe, we must be aware of the driving forces. When we are co-creating with the universe, we are sending signals to the cosmos, now if what we say we want doesn't match the frequency of that we say we want the universe will simply reflect the mixed signal sent back at us, which often gives what one asks for but also brings with it that which we didn't ask for. For example, let's say you are saying you are healthy, your words you speak of health but held deep within there is a core belief which says that you inherit health issues through DNA and that you have a mental illness because your parents passed it on, now what is happening is although you are saying you are healthy, you are in fact creating images of illness in mind which is being driven by the core belief that illness is in your DNA, and so although you speak the words, the actual frequency is out of alignment of that statement and so the universe just gives back what it receives and so in this case it would be the experience of either staying ill or creating illness.

When co-creating with the universe you must be clear on what you want, forget what you don't want, just be clear on your desire, the more clear you are with your images and emotions the more easier the universe can deliver to you want your heart desires.

I want to point out here that the universe doesn't understand words such as **'don't'** whenever we use the word 'don't' in metaphysical creation the universe picks this up as **'want'** this is why both wanting and not wanting hold equal power of manifestation.

The universe goes off images and emotion, so when you say something like "I hope I don't get another bill through the door" what is actually happening is subconsciously you are creating an image in your mind of receiving a bill through the door, which gives you the fearful feeling of receiving one then from that image a corresponding emotion which matches the frequency of fearing the bill coming through the door is created within the energy field which is then broadcast to the universe and thus the universal genie begins co-creating with you the experience of 'receiving a bill through the door

Whenever you are thinking, what you are doing is simply creating images in the mind, it is from these images where feelings arise whether positive or negative.

For example, when we say, "I am happy," we feel happy because through using imagination we are simply creating a positive image in our minds, the longer we stay in this energy, the happier experiences and thoughts the Universe sends to us because it is just a mirror of the inner (thoughts) images and feelings.

Because of this unconsciousness law of creation and the distorting of the power of the imagination or imagicreation as I like to call it, we have created and continue to create many thoughts and experiences that we don't enjoy. "I am" has the power to create not just our grandest dreams but also our worse fears.

I often say words are spells, so use them wisely. Words hold their own power. Think about how many times a certain word has made you feel good or bad. They have an effect, just like the water test shown in the media and government chapter.

We must remember that when using this powerful phrase, we should use it only with positive energy. By doing so, we will bring more of the positiveness we are stating into reality.

"I am" is the main reason why we find ourselves in much mental disarray. We are unknowingly attaching and identifying ourselves to those negative aspects, which is okay. I'm not saying you won't or can't feel down, low, or upset, I'm simply pointing out that you can experience those emotions without attaching or identifying yourself with that negative thought. Remember, thoughts are simply that: thoughts. We have sixty thousand thoughts a day and always have the power to change them.

We think so much that it's no wonder we are in mental turmoil. Who wouldn't be creating those images, linking themselves to all those thoughts and then attaching themselves emotionally to every thought? We need to remove any attachment or identifying with those negative statements. Yes, you can feel them, and you will. But once we start to remove the association with those negative feelings and experiences, we can use the power of words and thoughts for good. With time and training, we can remove those negative aspects of our realities and allow ourselves to quickly overcome any negative thoughts.

We can only overcome negative thoughts by making positive "I am" statements. For example, positive affirmation programming uses this formula. By continually saying "I am" and then "happy or joyous," or "abundant," for example, you will eventually cause yourself to see, feel, and experience yourself positively.

When it comes to those negative thoughts, there are two things we can do:

1. We can pass those thoughts to the angels and acknowledge that those negative thoughts have no power. We can do so by creating an affirmation stating that negative words have no power and that only positive statements hold power.

2. When we do feel or think something negative, we can take away our self-identification with it. We can use the pronoun "one" instead. For example, instead of saying, "I am feeling lonely," we can say, "one is seeing a cloud of loneliness right now, but this too shall pass," taking away the self-identification with that negative feeling and, thus, its power.

I know it may seem weird at first, and you may feel judged, but stick with it. When you use these strategies, you are detaching yourself from those negative thoughts or emotions and, thus, removing their power. Why do you think rich people refer to themselves as "one"? They know the secret of the power "I am."

Train yourself to reserve "I am" for positive thoughts and statements only. Doing so can bring about better health in the mind and body and help to create new experiences of joy and those that you want to experience. Also, over time and with training, it stops the negative self-talk; negative self-talk is what is causing many of the mental and physical issues we see today in the collective and individual consciousness of humanity.

I teach this technique in my courses. I gave to one of my students, and within a couple of weeks, the student was healed of anxiety and had begun to create more positive emotions and experiences. This change can happen in all areas of your life, be it wealth, health, confidence, experiences, or thoughts. Over time, it will help you rewire negative thought processes so that you can live a happier, healthier life and be more aligned with your soul.

The Message on I AM

When we are creating, we are using a combination of believe and emotion.

When we saying we are thinking what we are really doing is simply creating images subconsciously, from these images derives the emotion. E-motion, thoughts in motion.

The words I am hold a special power, it is like you rubbing the lamp of the universe and asking the universal genie to fulfill that statement, so whatever follows the I am statement and is held with faith, belief and focus will come to manifestation .

The universe doesn't understand words like we do, so words such as "**don't**" it dismisses, and sees it as "**want**" so be sure to keep your wishes in alignment with that which you positively want.

It is possible to re-program your imprinted images pressed upon the subconscious mind but repeating positive affirmations and using your imagicreation to create an image of what you desire.

The Universal Laws

In this chapter, we will go through the universal laws and explain what they mean for us on a soul level. You will come to notice how everything this book directly correlates with these laws.

It is my heartfelt belief that universal laws should be taught in the educational system if we want to eliminate much of today's confusion, bring to light the talent the world needs, and eliminate the many issues we notice today. Once we understand these laws and how they have been contributing to our reality. We can start to use them in correspondence with our highest good, change our realities, and bring clarity to the issues we have created, which will bring healing and bring us back into alignment with our true essence.

1. The Law of Mentality

The law of mentality implies everything in the universe is a mental creation of the Great Spirit, that all life, matter, and energy are thoughts extending from the mind of the Great Spirit and, therefore, our lives are simply an extension of our thoughts and core believes. Beliefs are derived from repetitive thoughts, which are often what we have been told and not what we have discovered. We are one great consciousness experiencing life. We experience things ow we think we will experience them. What we believe becomes true in our reality.

Examples from Everyday Life

Two people see a color. One says it is green, and the other says it's blue. To the soul, whatever is believed will be created in its personal reality. Therefore, each person sees the color as they believe it is, regardless of the collective. The phrase "believing is seeing" fits nicely here.

2. The Law of Correspondence

The law of correspondence states that everything we experience in our realities is a mirror of our inner selves created by our most-prominent inner thoughts. As Buddha said, "What we believe and conceive, we will achieve."

This law states that the external world is a reflection of our internal worlds. We create in our personal experiences the things we believe about ourselves and hold inside. If you are calm and peaceful inside, you will create that experience on the outside, but if you are filled with chaos and unhappy thoughts, your personal reality will also be chaotic and full of unhappy experiences.

Examples from Everyday Life

If you held strong prominent beliefs that you are a rich person, then you would find evidence of this in your reality. You would be perceived as being rich in finance, health, and opportunities. The same can be said of the opposite.

3. Law of Vibration

The law of vibration states that everything in the universe vibrates—that everything is in constant motion. Despite how we may perceive it on the material plane, nothing is solid, and everything has its own vibrational frequency. A brick, a phone, a car: these things only take on these forms because of the unique vibrational frequency signature they emit.

This law refers to not only material things but also the unseen. Thoughts, beliefs, and emotions emit their own unique vibrational frequencies. Positive thoughts of joy and peace emit a high frequency, and negative thoughts of stress and scarcity emit a low frequency.

We could also apply the law of attraction here. We attract the same frequencies that we predominately emit through our thoughts and beliefs. We are the creators of our realities, and what we put into the universe through our predominate thoughts (energy), we get back. When you understand the law of vibration, you will understand the law of attraction. Love attracts love, and fear attracts fear.

Examples from Everyday Life

Scientists have found that the things we perceive to be solid are actually dashing atoms filled with nothing but space. It is our minds that fill the space. Remember, everything is mental the law of mentality).

Here's another good example. When moving at high speeds, a tire looks like it is motionless. The same can be said about a stone—it appears to be solid and stagnant, but that's only because it is vibrating at a low level. Its particles are vibrating so slowly that they appear to be at rest.

4. The Law of Polarity

The law of polarity states that everything has a polar opposite. Hot and cold are the same—they are identical in nature—but different in degree. For one thing to exist, its opposite must also exist. For instance, let's take water. Water is simply water. Hot water is water but with a high vibrational frequency, whereas cold water is water but with a low vibrational frequency. Both are water but with different vibrational degrees.

Examples from Everyday Life

I often say that if it weren't for the darkness, we would not know light. For light to exist, there must be darkness. How would we know that a light bulb lights up the room if there wasn't a dark room to test it in? For us to know what is, there needs to be what is not. Opposites are the same but differ in degree. This can be applied to everything in the universe.

5. The Law of Rhythm

The law of rhythm states that everything flows with rhythm, and what goes around comes around. Everything that rises equally falls. Something that swings to the right will equally swing to the left. That which expands will contracts. The seasons and the body's aging process all move with rhythm.

It is often said that if you want to know the future, look to the past. The universe moves in cycles. Things get repeated. Rhythm is movement, movement is flow, flow is energy, and energy is life.

The tide of the sea goes out, but due to the law of rhythm, it comes back in, and so it carries on for eternity. On a soul level, that's what we do. Through experiences, growth, and enlightenment, we expand, and when it's time for inner contemplation, we retract our energy as we digest everything we have discovered. Once it's been digested, we expand again. This process is the continuous flow of life, the ebb and flow of the cosmos.

Examples from Everyday Life

Look at the waves in the ocean, the scale of a beating heart, the rhythm of human emotions, or the process of breathing. The level of the breath you draw in equals the level of breath your push out.

6. The Law of Neutralization

The law of neutralization states that although everything follows a rhythm, it's not necessarily experienced on the conscious plane. The universal laws are simply that: laws. You cannot change them, but you can use them to your advantage. This is where the law of neutralization comes in.

The law of neutralization allows us to choose if we consciously feel the swing. Yes, by universal law, happiness swings to sadness and back again, but we can choose where we focus our attention. On the subconsciously plane, the pendulum may swing to sadness, but on the conscious plane, we can neutralize the swing and bring it back to happiness by focusing on the happiness, so it seems as though the swing to sadness doesn't exist.

This work is not easy. It takes practice and self-mastery, but it is not impossible.

7. The Law of Cause and Effect

The law of cause and effect implies that everything in life has a cause and an effect, and every effect has a cause. Nothing is by chance. Your thoughts, behaviors, and actions create specific effects that manifest and create your life as you know it. Karmic energy is also a result of this law.

Let's quickly review what karma is. Despite what we have been taught, karma is not debts we need to repay. Karma is simply purposely recreated energy that comes in the form of an event or situation sent to you by the soul so that you can get a deeper and clearer picture of who you truly are. Karma can be the cause or effect, but we are not aware of them. For instance, let's say in one lifetime, you were a rich, healthy person who looked down and others who weren't as wealthy and treated them as lesser than you. This treatment then caused someone to commit suicide. You were the cause of the effect of suicide. In the next life, you are treated as the lesser than, and you commit suicide; thus, you experience the effect of the cause. Karma allows us to experience and bring full understanding to that which we may have misunderstood previously.

It's important to know that there is positive karmic energy, too. Positive karmic energies are events or situations that bring a dream, a goal, or a positive experience to fruition. These energies are mostly set when creating the soul plan before reincarnating for the purposes of soul growth and understanding.

We either create our lives according to what we desire (be the cause) or live a life someone else desires (the effect), which is what most people do these days—they live a life effects of the causes of the powers that be. You can choose if you create your life reality or if you are simply an effect of someone else's chosen reality. You can be unhappy because someone has told you to be, or you can be happy because you chose to be. You can be the ripple in the pond or the stone that caused the ripple.

Examples from Everyday Life

Let's say you have been conditioned to believe that you are unloved. This idea becomes a core belief and predominate thought, so you create this experience of being unloved in your reality, meaning you have become an effect of the cause. To become the cause of the effect, you would change that belief to the belief that you are loved. Once this belief replaces the belief that you are unloved, you will have moved from being the effect to being the cause.

Experience life how you wish to perceive it, not how you are told to perceive it. Either way, you become one or the other. The choice is always yours.

8. The Law of Gender

The law gender states that everything has both masculine and feminine qualities. As we discussed earlier, males hold female energy, and females hold male energy. Neither is Ying and Yang, but they are the Ying and Yang combined. This law applies not only to human anatomy but to everything in the universe. Everything has male and female qualities within it.

When we understand this law, we know that it is only natural (literally) for a person of one gender to express opposite gender tendencies. That is what it means to be in balance.

Examples in Everyday Life

We have already spoken about the effects of the cause of repression of the expression of opposite gender traits, but let's recap. It is perfectly okay for a man to cry, show emotion, or be compassionate, and it is perfectly okay for a woman to use her logic and masculine strength. When the soul remembers this law, it will uncover its own opposite energies and integrate them into its physical gender. All men have female energy, so it is perfectly acceptable for them to express this energy without judgment. All women have male energy, so it is perfectly acceptable for them to express this energy without judgment.

The Law of One

Those are the main laws. But although they seem like eight separate laws, they are, in fact, one big law. If you look at the list, you will see that they go hand in hand. If one law were missing, the rest would fail. That is why these laws are sometimes referred to as the law of one. I have combined all eight laws in a sequence below to give you a better understanding of how they work and relate to each other.

Everything is mental. The world we perceive is being created by our minds (the law of mentality). Everything we perceive in our reality is a reflection of our inner selves (the law of correspondence). If we feel good, then we have good external experiences. If we feel not so good, then we have not-so-good external experiences. The vibration of the predominate thoughts (the law of mentality + the law of correspondence + the law of vibration) will determine what we attract into our realities (the law of attraction).

Everything has its own vibrational frequency. The more pleasant emotions, such as happiness and contentment, are higher in frequency compared to more unpleasant emotions, such as hurt and depression. Although happiness and sadness are different in frequency, they are alike in nature and, thus, not separate (law of mentality). They are just at different degrees on the scale (the law of polarity).

Everything must have its opposite because two opposites make a whole. You can't have one without the other—you can't have summer without winter (the law of rhythm)—but you can choose how you perceive it (the law of correspondence). To see the positive in both (the law of vibration), you just need positive focus (the law of mentality + the law of correspondence) and the intention to move out the lower vibrational emotions and into the higher vibrational emotions (the law of vibration), knowing that the pendulum may swing but a that you can neutralize it (the law of neutralization) so that it only occurs on the subconscious plane. Consciously, you can remain at a high frequency. You are not allowing yourself to be the effect of the cause of the swing but allowing yourself to be the cause of the effect of the swing into happiness and the cause of your reality (the law of cause and effect). To do so best is to embrace both male and female energies (the law of gender) because embracing both aspects bring true balance. When we are in complete balance, we can better understand the universe and the laws of the universe (the law of mentalism).
And so, the cycle continues.

The Message on the universal laws

The universal laws govern all in the universe, none is exempt.

Although there are seven laws mentioned here, in hindsight it is just one law, this has been known as the law of one.

The laws have been known by scientist, philosophers and religious people alike.

By Understanding these laws you will have the keys to the universe, you will begin to see how everything came to be, and also how we can use this new knowledge of the laws to better the individual and collective experience upon earth.

The Stone and Ripple Effect

"Be the change you wish to see." —Gandhi

This chapter is about how simply making changes in your life creates a cosmic reaction to everything.

As we have already mentioned, we are all one—we are all part of the cosmic web—and for every action, there is a reaction. When a person decides to wake up—that is, become aware of the essence of their nature—it has a ripple effect. That is why I call it the stone and ripple effect. As one person wakes up, it causes another to awaken due to the cosmic connection we have with one another.

As we start to raise our vibrations, the things around us also start to change. A good example of this when you find yourself feeling low, and then a good friend comes around and cheers you up. Even if you don't necessarily want to be cheered up, you can't help but smile, and that is enough to bring that vibration up.

The thing is that when we find ourselves interacting with a higher vibration, it, in turn, raises our own vibrations. Higher vibrations have a more powerful effect than low vibrations. It has been scientifically proven by the rod test, which you can find on the internet. This test proves that positive thoughts have a wider and more powerful effect and that we pick them up more easily than we do lower vibrations.

As we focus on raising our vibration through various techniques (such as those mentioned in this book and by other awesome souls), we start to raise the vibration of those around us. That is why I say don't try to change the world but be the change you want to see. It will shake the cosmic web and cause others to wake up to who they are. As they awaken, they will cause others and so forth. So, you see, be that which you wish to create.

If you want to create love in your earthly experience, then be love. If you want to create wealth, then see yourself as and feel wealthy. As you start to change your earthly experiences, bringing more positivity, joy, and happiness, others will become curious. They will start to change their perspectives and, in turn, their perception. Even those who once feared or mocked you may confide in you about the changes they are experiencing or simply express their truth. That is just awesome! After all, we are all here to elevate one another and help one another grow and expand. If there weren't anyone to help, then you wouldn't have the experiences we have on Earth.

A point to remember when it comes to the stone and ripple effect is that it is similar to the combination of all the spiritual laws. You not only have an effect on those around you but will also attract great things to you. As you awaken people, you show more light in yourself, which brings more light to you. You get back what you give. As you knowingly or unknowingly help, support, and raise another's vibration through thoughts, words, and actions of love, compassion, harmony, unity, and joy, the Universe sees this act and gifts you more loving experiences, more reasons to be joyful, and more delightful surprises. That is what I would call anybody's heaven!

The Message about the Stone and Ripple Effect

What you chose to be will be reflected at you. The individual changes you make will affect the collective consciousness, and those upon your soul tree.

What we do to ourselves we do for others; we are connected through the cosmic web.

When we heal and forgive ourselves and others, this allows and creates space for forgiveness and healing to occur to others without physically interacting with them.

As you change so will the people in your human experience

The Golden Age

The reason why souls incarnate or reincarnate in times of upheaval or what seems like chaos is that they are times in which a golden age is due to start, much like the times we are in now.

Golden ages allow souls or groups of souls to accelerate in remembrance of their essence. Souls can jump through soul stages more quickly than they can at other times, so many souls chose to come to Earth during these times. Rather than having to reincarnate over many lifetimes to get from a young soul stage to an old soul stage, they chose a golden age in which there are plenty of experiences and opportunities available so that they skip many stages and go straight to a higher understanding and, thus, closer to soul fulfillment.

The reason for the creation of golden ages, such as the one we are entering and those that have come many times before, is so that those souls who were so lost can finally find their way home. The golden age is a phase in which souls can quickly advance in their remembrance.

During golden ages, the height of vibration reaches its peak, allowing souls to access higher vibrations and the vibration and place of where our wisdom lies. It allows souls to advance or graduate from the lower vibrations or dimensions onto the higher.

As mentioned in the chapter on the universal laws, everything follows a rhythm. What goes up must come down, and that goes for civilizations, too. Every civilization gets too a point of great advancement right before it drops back down to its lower stages. It is during these times of great advancement that souls can graduate from Earth.

Souls that have come to Earth are here to fulfill their soul plans. Once they have experienced everything they need to in this dimension, they move on to the higher realms, which is the goal of all souls. Golden ages are the perfect times to move on to the next realm.

The thing about the golden age we are in now and others we have seen before is that Earth has not only switched into a feminine energy but also moved in a new location cosmically. We are now in a new higher vibration that the old density we have experienced couldn't handle, so many of the lower energies and experiences are showing themselves to us both individually and collectively. Earth has reached a stage of evolution in which past energies that have dominated, and controlled humanity are losing their grip, and they know it.

Earth has hit a new level of energy and understanding. Remember, the creation of Earth and its freewill were an experiment, so once these experiences are seen from the higher vibrational perspective and healed, they will no longer be created. Now is the time when all that needs to be healed individually and collectively is going to be healed. Earth is about to jump into a new dimension, and it is urging us all to ascend with her.

Not all souls will join in this ascension. In fact, the majority will continue on a similar Earth but in a different galaxy and dimension. This change will not be known or felt by those souls that don't ascend with Earth. They will be none the wiser. But the cosmic seeds know that this leap is upon us, and the reason for them being here is to help bring the healing to each and every soul. Whether we chose to go with Earth or not, it is going, and there's no stopping it. That is why the Great Spirit, the angels, and I are bringing this book to your hands now and why many of the traumas are being urged toward release and healing.

The Great Spirit, your soul, the angels want you to ascend out of the density of the third dimension and join the realm of the fifth, where life will be as we know it here now. It will be a place and planet of great spiritual teachings and Divine love in a way we couldn't even dream. We can't fathom the amount things that will change and be different, so to simplify, Earth will be heaven—or should I say, there will be heaven on Earth.

That is where we are all heading. That is why the angels are coming in stronger than ever and why the intergalactic councils, federations, and other HEBs (higher evolved beings) are working with us and wanting so intensely for us to work with them. That is why the veil is dropping more than ever and why there is such a soul urge for each and every one of us to heal, release, and align with the soul, love, and essence. All this work is just preparation for the ascension.

Spiritual Tips

A lot of these tips have been around for a long, long time. You can always research on your own and find out what suits you best. We may all be one consciousness, but we are different, so we all have different perspectives and, thus, different ways of doing things. Some suit us, and some don't. There is no right or wrong way to do your rituals.

One of the things I find really helps to keep me centered and flowing with whatever the day may present me with is to meditate first thing in the morning, preferably out of my bed and outside. Being out with the breeze on my face and absorbing the high energy rays of the sun just settles my body easier.

To meditate like I do, settle down in whatever way suits you, be it seated on a chair or lying down. Just make sure you are comfortable. Before you go into your meditation, set your intention, whether it's to ground, cleanse, create, or anything else. Having an intention allows you to send your creative energies toward that which you wish to create with more power.

In the morning, I set an intention for the archangels and ascended masters to cut any cords that may be attached from this lifetime or any other for the highest good of myself and all in the universe. I intend to be guided by my higher self and the angels throughout the day to bring me joy and blessings, as well as to those around me and around the world. I call upon my angel guides, and then I focus on what I see my day being like. Again, this goes back to creation through thought (the law of attraction). Then I just sit quietly with a smile and my intentions in my heart.

I also meditate in the evening, and I set different intentions than I set in the morning. Because I am an oracle or angel card reader, I use this meditation to focus on whatever message I got in the cards or the image, breathing it in.

I'll admit that I am quite strict on myself. I always focus on the angelic and ascended-master energies around me on the given day.

These are all just ideas. You will find and your own intentions. It doesn't matter if your intentions change daily. As you grow, expand, and change, so will your intentions.

I also use affirmations. Affirmations are just positive statements repeatedly played, normally with some soothing or binaural music or beats. They simply remind me of who I am, what can be done, and what I can achieve. Remember, it's all about raising your energy. It has also been proven (and I am can say through my own experience) that listening to and repeating affirmations enough and really does start to rewire those negative core beliefs. It's is not going to happen overnight, and it will take discipline and persistence. Take responsibility and put the effort in, and you will experience the changes in your own reality.

Remember that "I am" is a power statement to the Universe, and with enough energy behind them, the words that follow will be created, so keep your "I am" statements positive. If negative thoughts or feelings come in, remove the "I am" and refer to yourself in the third person, using "one" or your name. Doing so strips away the identification with that thing. The more you use positive "I am" statements, the more your brain will start to use these words, too.

You can't affect or do anything to anyone without their permission, but you can hold a positive vision, meaning that if you wish something for someone, you can hold the vision for that person and help create the outcome they desire. This falls under grace (the law of cause and effect), so it can only be used for positive intentions. Any negative intentions will only be reflected back at you.

You can use vision boards. I have a couple hung in my room. Vision boards are boards with positive messages and images of the thing you want to create. This book is an example. The images can include whatever you wish, and it is best to combine those images with your meditations.

Binaural beats are a great way to relax and eventually access certain mental states. Research them to find out more.

I read positive books and have crystals and positive messages pinned around my room or office. These things give off high-frequency energy, and as I mentioned earlier, positive energy affects all our energy fields.

I choose my time of solitude. Make sure you balance your spiritual and earthwork.

Exercise is not just for synthetics but does wonders for the aura. It helps cleanse and align your mind, body, and spirit. But only light exercise. Overdoing it can do more harm than good to your body and your being. Again, everything in balance.

A balanced diet is a great way to keep yourself ground and aligned.

Treat yourself. Every month, I treat myself to something, whether it's a film or a day out. Whatever it is, treat yourself. You deserve it! It reminds you that you matter, and that joy is your purpose. Plus, it feels good!

Stay away from negative outlets, be they people or the media. Again, it will depend on what karmic energy you have and the lessons your soul is understanding—you may require a negative experience to fully understand a positive. This goes back to the idea that one doesn't exist without the other and that everything is a part of the whole experience, but if you don't need to be in that energy, then peel away soon as possible.

Take five minutes in the day, whether at home or work, to ground yourself and breathe. The day can present us with all sorts of challenges. Taking a moment to re-center will help you deal with things positively and see all that is as it is.

Clothing and colors affect our auras. I always check in to see what kind of day it is, whether its white, grey, or blue. However, everything is in relation to the context. For example, if you have a bit of temper, wearing a lot of red can increase that vibration because it's associated with the fire element, so it's best to wear blues or greens. Similarly, if you have your head in the clouds all the time, wearing red can help ground you. What we are given by Infinite Spirit will be in the context of what you have asked for. If you struggle to open your heart, wearing a bit of pink or green can help to open it; both are associated with the heart space. Again, everything is vibration, and the reason why we see things as different colors is that their vibrational frequencies are different.

Balance out your tunes. Find new high vibrational bands and music and balance out your pop, rap, or whatever music you vibe too with soft sounds. Music speaks to the soul.

Get out into nature. Take time to go for a walk or hike or to simply sit down. This helps relax the mind and soothe mental stress and chatter. It's also great for grounding.

Check-in with the guides, angels, and ascended masters. Simply focus on the being and thank them for whatever it is you feel they are supporting and guiding you with. This not only helps bring in the energy of the angels but also helps t build your connection with the angels and higher beings so that you can hear and feel their messages more clearly.

Another way to keep your mind in balance is to clean your home or workspace. I often say your home and workspace represent your mind space, so if your room or desk is cluttered, it often represents a cluttered mind. To help declutter the mind and quiet the monkey in the brain, clean your room or desk. Having a clean and tidy bedroom when you wake and go to bed and having a clean, clear space when you enter your living space will also raise your vibrations and help keep you centered. The more you clean your living spaces, the more you clear your mind will be. This is the basic principle of feng shui.

One last thing to remember is that you deserve space, so make sure you have at least an hour or two a day when you can do whatever you please: watch a TV show, visit family or friends, or do something else just for you. This tip is more for people in relationships. Too many people make their worlds small when they get into a relationship. Again, it's all about balance.

Final Words

I just want to thank you for taking the time to read this book, but more so for taking the time to remember who you truly are and what you are here to do. I know this journey can be difficult and hard at times, but you are amazing, wonderful, strong and more than capable to succeed in all your soul's lessons.

Continue to be change you wish to see and never give up on your individual journey of self-discovery.

If you need help don't be afraid to ask! The angels, your friends and family are all around you, if your human family isn't, know that your soul family Is! You have the potential to create whatever you wish, to be who you want to be, to look how you want to look, to attract what you want to attract, this is your own blank manifestation canvas it is time you use it for the love of yourself, so for you to heal those past experiences and create space for new experiences. I hope that this book has helped you to understand on a basic foundational level the purpose of you, your soul, experiences and your journey.

May we all help to heal one another, may we come together and realize our oneness with each and all, through this oneness bring back into balance and alignment our divine essence, to heal ourselves, others and the universe of all previous cosmic karma, to make way for the new world.

Thank you for joining me and the angels and the universe in this divine invitation, may you grow and align. Please share this book with others and pass the message on.

All my heart and love Lee

www.ingramcontent.com/pod-product-compliance
Lightning Source LLC
Chambersburg PA
CBHW030759150426
42813CB00068B/3252/J